EXPLORI[ ]

Blaenavon Industrial World Heritage Site

EXPLORING
Blaenavon Industrial Landscape
World Heritage Site

Chris Barber

BLORENGE BOOKS

First published 2002

ISBN 1 872730 26 4

All photographs are by Chris Barber FRGS
Illustrations by Michael Blackmore

BLORENGE BOOKS

Blorenge Cottage, Church Lane, Llanfoist, Abergavenny, Gwent NP7 9NG
Tel: 01873 856114

Printed by MWL Print Group Ltd,
Units 10/13, Pontyfelin Industrial Estate, New Inn,
Pontypool, Torfaen NP4 ODQ
Tel: 01495 750033

ACKNOWLEDGEMENTS

I am most grateful to everyone who has assisted me with the production of this book which is the result of many years of research and exploration. Special thanks are due to my good friend Michael Blackmore for his excellent illustrations and genuine enthusiasm for the project. I also thank Dr John van Laun for his advice and observations on the draft manuscript. Richard Keen, I warmly thank for writing the Foreword.

My grateful appreciation is also given to the staff of several libraries, particularly the Librarian of the Dobel-Moseley Library and Archive of Pontypool Museum.

Ann Waller I thank for proof reading the final manuscript and I am particularly grateful to John Rodger, the Blaenavon World Heritage Site Project Officer for all his help and encouragement.

This book has been published with financial assistance from Torfaen County Borough Council, Monmouthshire County Council, Brecon Beacons National Park Authority, Wales Tourist Board and Blaenavon Town Council.

Blaenavon Town Council

There are two major preserved industrial sites, Blaenavon Blast furnaces, and the Big Pit Mining Museum. There are also substantial survivals of housing and other buildings associated with an urban lay-out that is characteristic of this type of industrial settlement. What is also interesting is the relationship of this industrial area with the undisturbed rural landscape lying just a few miles to the north, which demonstrates dramatically how industry was implanted in the late eighteenth century.

Dr Henry Cleere
World Heritage Co-ordinator

CONTENTS

Richly endowed with woodland, water, limestone and ironstone of excellent quality, it is little wonder that Blaenavon became an early centre of the iron industry.

T.G. Grey Davies

FOREWORD

As an enthusiast who has been shouting about the special qualities of the industrial heritage of South Wale for a long time it is such a pleasure to see the inclusion of the Blaenavon Industrial Landscape in the World Heritage list.

Our industrial heritage can have an important role in the 21st century as part of wider regeneration schemes. The outstanding work by Torfaen County Borough Council and other members of the Blaenavon Partnership has preserved an important area of landscape and changed perceptions of industrialisation and its history.

Important names feature in the Blaenavon story. Sidney Gilchrist Thomas and Percy Gilchrist are two. But what gives the place such significance for me is the fact that Big Pit, the remains of the ironworks, the network of tramroads, watercourses and reservoirs, the spectacular quarries and that massive area of twisted, torn, prodded and probed landscape dominating the skyline above the town are enduring memorials to the role of the great unsung of history. The countless numbers of people who lived around the mines, quarries and ironworks were some of the true makers and creators of Britain as the first industrialised nation in the world. Every shovelful of coal, every pig of iron contributed to this great endeavour.

For most people who came into the area in the late 18th and early 19th centuries, from far and wide, it was a step into the unknown. They were the first generation to make the transition from a rural to an industrial economy. The coming of industry was momentous, and ultimately changed the face of the greater part of the globe. Those people were the pioneers in so many ways. When I stand inside the cottages at Stack Square or walk along Hill's Tramroad to the iron forge at Garnddyrys I try to imagine what those early industrial workers experienced. Their lot was that of hard work, difficult conditions and, more often than not, a poor and short life. Gender and age were of little consequence. In the iron works and the collieries could be found children under the age of ten and it was commonplace for women and men to be working well beyond our present retirement age.

The landscape that is the backdrop to this book is extraordinary. Blaenavon is an excellent example of a 19th century town that thankfully has retained so many of its important features including the quite magnificent Workingmen's Institute, St Peter's School and St Peter's Church alongside. To wander through the graveyard is to experience 'instant' social history from the inscriptions on the headstones and the school is of great significance as one of the earliest company schools in Wales.

From the top of the Blorenge the views are extraordinary, with the rich agricultural land around Abergavenny in one direction and the rolling upland plateau of the valleys in the other. The views are magnificent. The land is marked with the evidence of hundreds of years of human occupation; sometimes obvious like the great limestone quarries whereas elsewhere careful searching through the heather reveals a long abandoned watercourse leading to a dry reservoir. Everywhere you look and walk there is evidence of human endeavour and the steep slopes around Pwll Du are crisscrossed by tramroads clinging tenaciously to the contours before plunging precipitously down an incline to meet the quiet waters of the Brecon & Abergavenny Canal.

All that and more can be found in Chris Barber's wonderful companion and guide to this landscape. I thought I knew this particular patch fairly well until I read this book and used it in the field. I now have found out so many more features and improved my understanding of the various pieces that fit together to make the Blaenavon landscape jigsaw. The research and descriptions are magnificently enhanced by the vivid and expert 'recreations' of Michael Blackmore, his interpretations give life to the heritage.

This book carries on with the tradition that was started by Alexander Cordell when he wrote his best seller featuring the sites that now form part of the historic landscape. Above all it was Cordell who first drew popular attention to the rich human history of this part of the world, a history that is so clearly manifest in the landscape. It is entirely fitting that Chris Barber has written a book that gives us such access and insight to the people and their place. He has done so much to keep the work of Cordell in our minds.

It has been a pleasure to contribute, in a very small way, to singing the praises of a most remarkable part of the world at the interface of industrial and rural Wales. It was on landscapes such as this where the character of the society of South Wales was made.

Take time to explore this landscape and let this book and the sites tell their story.

Richard Keen

National Trust Welsh Culture
and Landscape Adviser
February 2002

INTRODUCTION

Between 1760 and 1840 a chain of ironworks were established along a narrow strip of hill country stretching for twenty miles between Blaenavon and Hirwaun, taking advantage of the rich deposits of ironstone, limestone and coal which were the essential materials required for the ironmaking process. This area at the 'Heads of the Valleys' of Southeast Wales was to become the most important iron making region in Britain and people seeking work came in their thousands from the rural areas of Wales, England and Ireland, attracted by the possibility of employment or higher wages.

For more than 150 years the collieries and ironworks of this part of Britain were of international significance but in recent years much of our industrial heritage has been swept away. Yet at Blaenavon can still be found the best preserved multi-blast furnace complex of its period and type in the world. Coal, fireclay and iron nodules were found together in the coal measures of the Afon Lwyd valley and the mountain top while fluxing stone was quarried in the limestone which lay a few kilometres to the north overlooking the Usk Valley.

The industrial landscape which surrounds Blaenavon provides a unique outdoor classroom for visiting educational parties, who study the complete story of ironmaking where study of the complete story of ironmaking is possible including the extraction of raw materials, furnace and forge technology, the development of early transport systems and the social history of the people who provided the workforce over a period of two hundred years.

It was Alexander Cordell's, famous novel 'Rape of the Fair Country', published in 1959, which brought to people's attention the historic importance of Blaenavon. When he sold the film rights to the book in 1960, the resultant publicity had the effect of saving the old ironworks and nearby Stack Square from destruction. Thankfully, the Blaenavon Town Council decided that these 'crumbling ruins' should not be bulldozed and levelled, but retained as a possible film set. Sadly, despite interest shown by the actors Stanley Baker and Richard Burton, the film has never been made, but now perhaps as a result of World Heritage designation, there is a greater chance of such a project being undertaken.

In the early 1990's when some thought was given to the Blaenavon Industrial Landscape as a possible World Heritage Site, Alexander Cordell commented that if this could be achieved it would be a fitting epitaph to the people who died making this small town such an industrial giant. "All that the people of the past have to commend them for the sacrifices they made, are the dirt monuments that they left behind. That is why it is so incumbent on people with influence to sacrifice everything to get this done. There is no town which deserves it better than Blaenavon"!

Thanks to the sterling efforts of the Blaenavon Partnership led by the Torfaen County Borough Council, Cordell's dream of World Heritage site status was realised on November 30th 2000. On this memorable day the World Heritage Committee of UNESCO inscribed the 'Blaenavon Industrial Landscape' on the list of World Heritage Sites.

When the former County of Gwent was divided into new smaller Unitary Authorities in 1996, the new Torfaen County Borough Council was determined to do something to regenerate the town of Blaenavon which had suffered greatly from the decline of the traditional coal and steel industries. The population of the town dropped from 12,500 in 1921 to about 6,000 persons in 1996. The older housing stock was in a generally poor state of repair and town centre shops were in a very run down condition.

In 1997 the Council hosted a major heritage conference at the Parkway Hotel Cwmbran, bringing together expertise in conservation and industrial archaeology from a wide range of bodies in the UK and beyond. The purpose of the conference was to consider the significance of Blaenavon's industrial landscape; whether it was appropriate to pursue World Heritage Site status and what this could mean in terms of the regeneration of the area. The question was posed: Could Blaenavon build a "future on the past"? The opinion of all the delegates was that Blaenavon could and should try to achieve regeneration based on its very special industrial heritage.

What makes Blaenavon so special is the fact that it has, surprisingly, been left virtually untouched by modernisation. The basic fabric of both the town and the surrounding landscape remains intact and provides one of the best preserved industrial landscapes in Britain. Not only does the area contain a large concentration of internationally significant archaeological features: but it provides a fascinating reminder of the important role the people of this part of Wales played in the formative years of the Industrial Revolution.

Following the conference, Torfaen County Borough Council assembled a partnership of interests to pursue World Heritage Site status and the regeneration of the area. The strength of the partnership was to result in truly remarkable progress to World Heritage status. The partnership comprises: Torfaen County Borough Council, Monmouthshire County Council, Blaenau Gwent County Borough Council, Brecon Beacons National Park, Blaenavon Town Council, Cadw, The Royal Commission for the Historic and Ancient Monuments of Wales, The National Museum and Galleries of Wales, The Countryside Council for Wales, The Welsh Development

Agency, The Wales Tourist Board, British Waterways and the National Trust. This strong Partnership of local authorities and agencies have been encouraged in their efforts from the beginning by the new National Assembly for Wales.

When in April 1999 Chris Smith, the Secretary of State for Culture, Media and Sport (DCMS) announced his long awaited final "tentative list" of 25 sites, the UK government wished UNESCO to add to the existing 18 World Heritage Sites in the UK, the Blaenavon Industrial Landscape figured on the list. Indeed the Blaenavon Industrial Landscape was the first site in the UK to be nominated in June 1999 and it was anticipated that the the other sites on the list would be over the following ten years.

After careful scrutiny the World Heritage Committee meeting at Cairns in Australia, inscribed the Blaenavon Industrial Landscape as a World Heritage Site on 30 November 2000. This was a tremendous achievement bearing in mind that over 500 sites in the UK had expressed a keen interest in being World Heritage Sites.

The Committee agreed:

"The area around Blaenavon bears eloquent and exceptional testimony to the pre-eminence of South Wales as the World's major producer of iron and coal in the 19th century. All the necessary elements can be seen in-situ, coal and ore mines, quarries, a primitive railway system, furnaces, the houses of the workers, and the social infrastructure of their community."

The Blaenavon Partnership is to be congratulated in achieving World Heritage status for the area. Not only is it one of the birthplaces of the Industrial Revolution and therefore worthy of preservation in its own right, but there is also potential to bring considerable economic benefit to the local community.

No less than 45% of this World Heritage Site lies within the Brecon Beacons National Park and while the industrial history is of special interest, it is undoubtedly the outstanding scenic quality of the landscape which provides an added bonus for the visitor.

To walk along the gently curving tramroad, named after the ironmaster Thomas Hill, around the side of the Blorenge Mountain, taking in the delightful views across the golden valley of the Usk, is a very satisfying experience. It is not unusual for the casual visitor to be so captivated by such scenery that a strong desire to return is firmly implanted.

Chris Barber
Llanfoist 2002

BLAENAVON INDUSTRIAL LANDSCAPE WORLD HERITAGE SITE

What is a World Heritage Site?

The World Heritage Convention was adopted by the UNESCO (United Nations Educational, Scientific and Cultural Organisation) in 1972 and has now been endorsed by 124 States. It provides for the inscription on the World Heritage List of natural and those sites "of outstanding universal value" to ensure their identification, protection, conservation, presentation and promotion, so that their significance can be appreciated by present and future generations. There are currently 721 World Heritage Sites of which only 33 are industrial sites.

Examples of other World Heritage Sites

Sites inscribed on the World Heritage list include such famous places as the Pyramids, the Taj Mahal, The Great Wall of China and Venice. Among the most famous natural sites are the Great Barrier Reef and the Grand Canyon. In Britain there are now 22 World Heritage Sites including Stonehenge, Hadrian's Wall, Westminster Abbey and Greenwich.

However, there has been a recent but growing awareness that Britain's greatest contribution to the development of the world was its leading role in the Industrial Revolution. Ironbridge Gorge often referred to as the birthplace of the Industrial Revolution was inscribed in 1986. The Blaenavon Industrial Landscape was inscribed in 2000 and reflects the growing trend in the awareness of contextual settings to monuments i.e. the concept of cultural landscapes.

In 2001 three other UK industrial sites were added to the World Heritage list. New Lanark, Saltaire and the Derwent Valley Mills, famous as the beginning of the factory system. The well known Dorset and Devon fossil coast was also inscribed as a natural site.

The total number of World Heritage Sites in Britain is now 22. However, it is anticipated that additions to the list will be limited to 30 per year and at most one per year will be added from UK over the next ten years or so, to redress the balance between the number of sites in Western Europe and the rest of the world.

The Blaenavon Initiative: Regeneration through Heritage

World Heritage Site status has been welcomed simply as recognition of the leading role that South Wales played in the production of iron and steel. However, the Blaenavon Partnership has always seen a key link between heritage and regeneration. The main aim of the partnership is:-

"To protect and conserve this landscape so that future generations may understand the contribution South Wales made to the Industrial Revolution. By presentation and promotion of the Blaenavon Industrial Landscape it is intended to increase cultural tourism and assist the economic regeneration of the area."

While World Heritage Site Status does not of itself bring any direct funding it has proved a catalyst to securing funding from the European Commission, The National Assembly for Wales, The Heritage Lottery Fund and other sources. Following inscription the fortunes of the town have begun to revive and already significant conservation works and economic regeneration has been achieved. Most importantly the community has begun to feel some of the confidence that made Blaenavon great in times past.

The old Council Office in the centre of Blaenavon
has been restored to provide a new library for the town

Boundary of the Blaenavon World Heritage Site

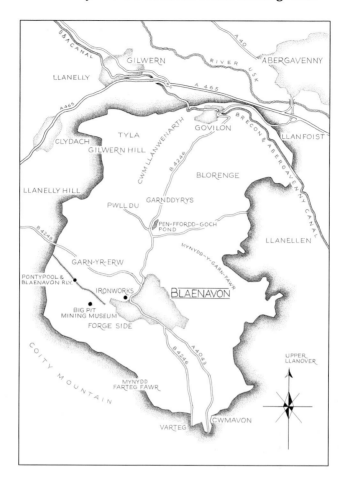

The boundary of the site is defined principally by the boundaries of land which was historically leased or purchased to provide the minerals and infrastructure for the Blaenavon Ironworks, and by additional land used in direct association with the Ironworks or its communities.

Measuring 8 kilometres north to south and 6 kilometres east to west the total area of the site is 32.9 square kilometres (3,290 hectares). The portion within the County Borough of Torfaen is 1804 hectares, and the area within Monmouthshire County Council is 1486 hectares. About 45% of the designated site falls within the Monmouthshire section of the Brecon Beacons National Park and comprises a mountain top landscape with a fall of 500m to the Monmouthshire and Brecon Canal.

Significance of the Blaenavon Industrial Landscape

✝ The area around Blaenavon is one of the best examples in the world of a landscape created by coal mining and ironmaking in the late eighteenth century and the early nineteenth century. The parallel development of these industries was one of the principal dynamic forces of the Industrial Revolution.

✝ When built in 1789, Blaenavon Ironworks with its three blast furnaces was one of the largest ironworks in the world. Today, this site is recognised as the best preserved blast furnace complex of its period and type in existence.

✝ Within a short distance of the ironworks can be found the sources of all its raw materials i.e. coal, iron ore and limestone. Extensive evidence can be seen on the hills surrounding Blaenavon, of the methods used to extract these raw materials during the fist decade of the operation of the ironworks.

✝ Linking the ironworks, the iron ore and coal workings, the quarries and wharves on the Brecknock and Abergavenny Canal is a fascinating network of primitive railways, including the longest tunnel in the world, constructed for horse-drawn operation.

✝ Big Pit, probably before 1860 and operated until 1980, is now the National Coal Mining Museum for Wales. It is one of only two coal mines in Britain where it is possible for visitors to descend in a pit cage and see authentic underground workings. As a key element in the industrial landscape of Blaenavon, Big Pit is also one of the essential features in the interpretation of the history of coal mining in the United Kingdom.

✝ The town of Blaenavon evolved near the head of the Afon Lwyd as a result of the establishment of the Ironworks and today it is rated as the finest example of a valley head town in South Wales. It is scheduled as a conservation area and contains many listed buildings of Special Architectural or Historic Interest. These include an ironmaster's house, a church and school built by the owners of the ironworks, examples of worker's housing, numerous chapels and an impressive Workmen's Hall and Institute. Such buildings all help to tell the story of the social development of the town over a period of two hundred years.

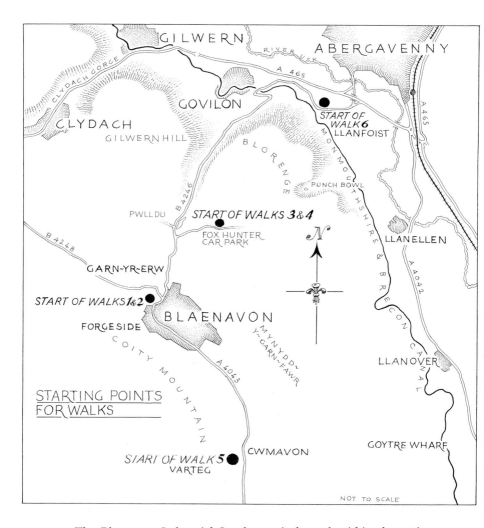

The Blaenavon Industrial Landscape is located within dramatic mountain scenery which attracts many casual visitors, by car, cycling and walking. Much of the site is within the Brecon Beacons National Park which is one of the most popular areas for walking holidays in the United Kingdom. The 'disturbed' industrial landscape offers a contrast with the traditional countryside and natural attractions of other areas within the National Park.

World Heritage Industrial Landscape
Nomination Document 2000

BLAENAVON IRONWORKS

In 1787 Thomas Hill, and Benjamin Pratt, two businessmen from the Stourbridge area in the Midlands of England, decided that Blaenavon was a suitable location to establish a new ironworks and were success-ful in negotiating the lease of 18 square kilometres of land from Lord Abergavenny. They were joined in their venture by Thomas Hopkins, the brother-in-law of Thomas Hill. He was a Welsh-speaking Welshman who had been a successful works manager in Rugeley, Staffordshire and was no doubt delighted to be given an opportunity to return to the land of his birth.

The first lease of land was dated 30th November 1788 and related to an area of moorland spread across seven parishes: Aberystruth, Trevethin, Llanhilleth, Goytre, Llanover, Llanfoist and Llanwenarth. The lease was to run for 21 years at £1,300 per annum, without royalties. It stated that Henry, Earl of Abergavenny 'granted the royalties, mines and minerals, coal and limestone, with power to work the same, and to erect furnaces thereon, in under and over 12,000 acres, commonly called Lord Abergavenny's Hill.'

Two years later these three entrepreneurs began operating their iron-works which built at a cost of £40,000 was the first purpose-built multi-furnace ironworks in Wales. As was general in South Wales they chose a site where their three furnaces could be built into a bank for ease of charging from above. At the foot of each furnace a casthouse was built. In keeping with the latest technology they decided to use a steam engine rather than water power to blast the furnaces: this was supplied by Boulton & Watt. Steam blowing was not exactly new having been used by John Wilkinson (1728-1808) near Broseley in Shropshire in 1776. This was also supplied by Boulton & Watt. Steam blowing freed ironmasters from the dependence on waterpower and gave some freedom of choice in locating blast furnaces.

In 1790 the three furnaces started producing pig iron which initially was transported by mule to Newport. Six years later the Monmouthshire Canal was opened between Newport and Pontnewynydd. This was linked with the Blaenavon Ironworks by a six mile railroad down the Afon Lwyd Valley.

Between 1790 and 1792 the works produced 3,600 tons of iron per annum and this output reached 5,460 tons by 1796. By this time the Blaenavon Ironworks was the largest producer of iron in Wales and ten years later output had been increased to 7,846 tons per year.

William Coxe accompanied by Sir Richard Colt Hoare paid his first visit to Blaenavon in 1799 and provided us with a useful description of the ironworks as it appeared after ten years of operation:-

At some distance, the works have the appearance of a small town, surrounded with heaps of ore, coal, and limestone, and enlivened with all the bustle and activity of an opulent and increasing establishment. The view of the buildings, which are constructed in the excavations of the rocks, is extremely picturesque, and heightened by the volumes of black smoke emitted by the furnaces. While my friend Sir Richard Hoare was engaged in sketching a view of this singular scene, I employed myself in examining the mines and works.

This spot and its vicinity produce abundance of iron, with coal and limestone, and every article necessary for smelting the ore; the veins lie in the adjacent rocks, under strata of coal, and are from three and a half to seven or eight inches in thickness; they differ in richness, but yield, upon an average, not less than forty-four pounds of pig iron to one hundred weight of ore. The principal part of the iron, after being formed into pigs, is conveyed by means of the rail road and canal to Newport, from whence it is exported.

The shafts of the mines are horizontal, penetrating one below the other, and under the coal shafts; iron rail roads are constructed to convey the coal and ore; which are pushed as far as the shafts are worked, and gradually carried on as the excavations are extended; the longest of these subterranean passages penetrates not less than three quarters of a mile. The coal is so abundant as not only to supply the fuel necessary for the works, but large quantities are sent to Abergavenny, Pont y Pool, and Usk.

Although these works were only finished in 1789, three hundred and fifty men are employed, and the population of the district exceeds a thousand souls. The hollows of the rocks and sides of the hills are strewed with numerous habitations, and the healthy ground converted into fields of corn and pasture. Such are the wonderworking powers of industry when directed by judgement!

The want of habitations for the increasing number of families, has occasioned an ingenious contrivance: a bridge being thrown across a deep dingle for the support of a railroad leading into a mine, the arches, which are ten in number, have been walled up, and formed into dwellings; the bridge is covered with a penthouse roof, and backed by perpendicular rocks, in which the mines are excavated. Numerous workmen continually pass and repass, and low cars, laden with coal or iron ore, roll along with their broad and grooved wheels; these objects, losing themselves under the roof of the bridge, again emerging, and then disappearing in the subterraneous passages of the rock, form a singular and animated picture, not unlike the moving pictures in a camera obscura.

The mountainous district which contains these mineral treasures, is held by the Earl of Abergavenny, under a lease from the Crown. It was formerly let to the family of Hanbury, of Pontypool, for less than £100 a year; and as the value of the mines was not sufficiently appreciated, no works were constructed; but the masses of ore found near the surfaces were conveyed to the forges of Pont y Pool. Soon after the expiration of the term, the district was granted by another lease to Hill and Company, who began these works in 1788, and expended forty thousand pounds before any return was made; this expense, however, has been amply repaid by the produce.

This engraving of Blaenavon Ironworks by William Byrne, based on a sketch by Sir Richard Colt Hoare, can be seen in William Coxe's *An Historical Tour in Monmouthshire* which was first published in 1801. The drawing was made in 1799 when the works was just ten years old but there is much of interest to be seen in the picture.

It shows three blast furnaces built against the cliff to enable easy charging from above. Between two of the furnaces is the blowing house, where a steam engine provided the blast and smoke can be seen rising from a tall round chimney. In front of the furnaces are the cast houses where the molten iron was run off into beds of sand to mould the lengths of pig iron (see page 32).

There is a wooden footbridge where the stone balance tower now stands and a team of mules with panniers can be seen carrying loads of raw material to the furnaces.

On considering the rise and rapid progress of the iron manufactories in this district, as well as in the neighbouring mountains of Monmouthshire and Glamorganshire, it is a matter of wonder that these mineral treasures should have been so long neglected. This wonder will increase, when it is known that iron was manufactured in this country at a period beyond the reach of tradition or history. Large heaps of slag or cinder have been repeatedly discovered, some of which are evidently the product of bloomeries, the most ancient method of fusing iron; in other places are traced the sites of furnaces long disused, of which no account of their foundation can be collected. The appearance of these iron cinders, and the vestiges of ancient furnaces, indicate that many parts of this mountainous district, now wholly bare, were formerly covered with large tracts of wood; charcoal being the only species of fuel originally used in the operation of smelting, both in the bloomeries and furnaces. This conjecture is corroborated by numerous names, alluding to woods and forests, in places which have never been known to produce trees; and is still farther ascertained by the discovery of trunks and branches, with their leaves, under the boggy soil in the vicinity of Blaenavon, and on the neighbouring hills.

The lands being cleared, and the forests neglected, their destruction was hastened by numerous herds of goats, maintained in these mountainous regions; the want of fuel occasioned the gradual decline of the bloomeries and furnaces, and for a considerable period little or no iron was manufactured.

About forty years ago the iron works suddenly revived, from the beneficial discovery of making pig iron with pit coal, instead of charcoal, which was soon afterwards followed by the improvement of manufacturing even bar iron by means of pit coal: hence a district, which contained such extensive mines of ore and coal, prodigious quantities of limestone, and numerous streams of water, could not fail of becoming the seat of many flourishing establishments. Besides these local advantages, the progress of the manufactories has been powerfully aided by the application of mechanics; particularly by the use of the steam engine, and the great improvement of water machines; but in no instance have they derived more advantage than from the adoption of rollers, instead of forge hammers, now used for the formation of bar iron, with a degree of dispatch, as well as exactness, before unknown. From this concurrence of circumstances, the success has been no less rapid than extraordinary: fifteen years ago the weekly quantity of pig iron made in this part of Monmouthshire, and in the contiguous district of Glamorganshire, did not exceed 60 tons; at present it scarcely falls short of 600; at that period no bar iron was manufactured; but now the quantity amounts weekly to more than 300 tons. The works are still rapidly increasing in extent and importance, and appear likely to surpass the other iron manufactories throughout the kingdom.

The works prospered considerably during the Napoleonic wars and in about 1810 two more furnaces (Nos 4 & 5) were added. A second engine house was also built. Today, of the three earliest furnaces, only the remains of No 1 survive, the other two having been demolished in the late nineteenth century.

Thomas Hopkins had died in 1789 and his place was taken by his son Samuel who was a popular man in Blaenavon. His death in 1816 was a sad loss to the town and the people mourned his passing. His quarter share of the works was bequeathed to Thomas Hill, junior and the works was now controlled absolutely by the Hills, father and son, who decided to diversify the business. Up until then it had been entirely in cast iron, and in 1817 a forge for the production of wrought iron goods was opened at Garnddyrys, on the north side of the Blorenge, which enabled the proprietors to take advantage of the lower tolls on the Brecknock & Abergavenny Canal.

This tablet commemorating Benjamin Pratt can be seen on the south wall of the nave in St Woolos Cathedral, Newport. A story is told of how his life came to an end one evening in 1795 when he was dining with a friend at the Angel Hotel in Abergavenny. He rose from his chair to ring for a waiter and on sitting down became very giddy. His friend heard him exclaim, 'I am going to die - but I die an honest man! ' He then collapsed and promptly died.

After the close of the Napoleonic Wars iron became increasingly important for non-military purposes, especially in the construction of railways, rolling stock, bridges etc. Exports grew, thus stimulating the use of iron in the shipbuilding industry.

Until the 1820s Blaenavon was one of the most important and productive iron-making centres in Britain. But in that year production began to decline and Thomas Hill was unable to raise the capital required for investment in new plant. He died in 1824, leaving his share of the works equally between his sons Thomas and Waldron, who continued to run the business. Thomas Hill Junior was an arrogant man who made himself unpopular with the workers and townsfolk. His extravagant lifestyle involved large amounts of drink and rich living, which shortened his life and by 1827 he too had passed away, leaving his eleven-sixteenths share to his 29 year old Eton educated son, also named Thomas. He ran the works with his uncle Waldon Hill until the latter retired from active participation in 1830. Thomas Hill then took on Robert Wheeley, the works manager as his partner. They ran the concern together until 1836 when Thomas Hill accepted an offer of £222,050 for the works from a consortium of London merchants and the Blaenavon Iron & Coal Co. was formed to take over the business, the capital being raised by an issue of 8,000 shares of £50 each. The formal Deed of Settlement was not executed until 1838 and in that year the control of the Hill family finally came to an end. (Thomas Hill III died in 1868 at Rudhall in Herefordshire). The new Company obtained a Royal Charter in April 1839 and William Unwin Sims, the chairman, was also a director of the Bristol and London Railroad (later renamed the Great Western Railway).

James Ashwell, a civil engineer from Nottinghamshire with experience of managing ironworks in Derbyshire and Scotland, was appointed Managing Director of the Blaenavon Iron & Coal Company and given the task of modernising the ironworks. In 1840 the travel writer Nicholson paid a visit to Blaenavon during his Tour of Wales and he was evidently impressed with the works, for he commented:

> *At the works of the Blaenavon Iron Company, five furnaces are all in blast, blown with cold air and six others erecting. This mineral property is one of the best and most valuable in the County of Monmouth, and these works have been distinguished for the superior strength and general excellence of their iron. These five furnaces produce about 400 tons of cast iron per week, about half of which is refined, and part of it made into cable iron, and the remainder is sold for tinplates and foundry work. This company is erecting extensive forges and rolling mills.*

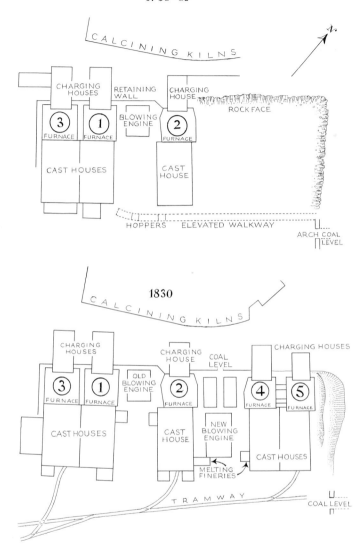

When viewed from Stack Square the furnaces numbered from left to right: 3, 1, 2, 4 and 5. This seemingly illogical way of numbering is marked on a plan drawn in 1814. The most complete furnace (dating from 1789) is No 2 and right up to 1902 it was still in use, producing high grade cold blast iron. Nos 4 and 5 furnaces (built in 1810) are also quite well preserved. But the hearths were altered in 1881 for the purpose of casting ingots which were used in steelmaking by the Gilchrist Thomas process at the Forgeside Works.

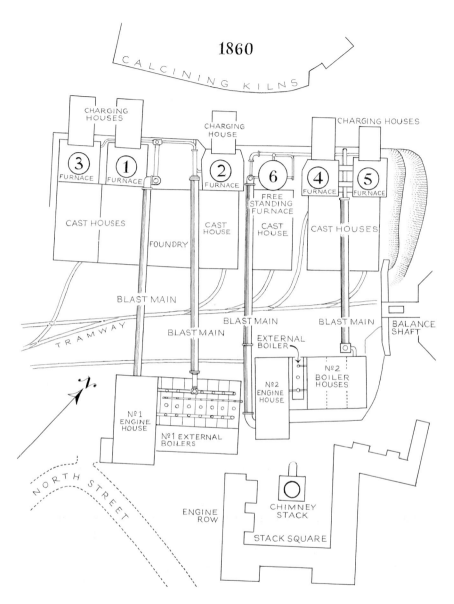

1860

CALCINING KILNS

CHARGING HOUSES

CHARGING HOUSE

CHARGING HOUSES

③ FURNACE ① FURNACE ② FURNACE ⑥ FREE STANDING FURNACE ④ FURNACE ⑤ FURNACE

CAST HOUSES

CAST HOUSE

CAST HOUSE

CAST HOUSES

FOUNDRY

BLAST MAIN

TRAMWAY

BLAST MAIN

BLAST MAIN

BLAST MAIN

BLAST MAIN

BALANCE SHAFT

EXTERNAL BOILER

Nº2 BOILER HOUSES

Nº2 ENGINE HOUSE

Nº1 ENGINE HOUSE

Nº1 EXTERNAL BOILERS

NORTH STREET

ENGINE ROW

CHIMNEY STACK

STACK SQUARE

Ashwell's plan was to build a new ironworks, with six blast furnaces, puddling furnaces and rolling mills on the other side of the valley below Coity Mountain and work began on this ambitious scheme. Before long the Company was in serious financial difficulty. Ashwell was heavily criticised at a meeting of the shareholders for committing the Company to what they no doubt considered a 'hair-brained' scheme and he duly resigned.

Following James Ashwell's departure, the works was put under the management of Harry Scrivenor on 1 January 1841. Work continued on the new furnaces but a slump in iron price the following year put a stop to such developments. During his period of employment at Blaenavon, Harry Scrivenor wrote a useful book entitled *History of the Iron Trade*. Unfortunately the works still failed to prosper and 1843 was a particularly disastrous year, as reported in the Monmouthshire Merlin :

> *The present state of the iron-trade annihilates hope, we see nothing but ruin before us and behind us. The trade must refine within its proper limits, but how is that to be effected - who are to stand, who are to fall - what is to become of the unemployed - how starvation is to be arrested, and the ruin of thousands averted - are questions beyond our provence to unravel, but which must be met boldly in our face, because they are not to be avoided - they are already at our door.*

At such times as this the workers suffered considerably and strife between them and the ironmasters became most bitter. However, an increased demand for iron rails in 1844 resulted in a substantial improvement in trade and profits for 1845 were most satisfactory. In about 1847 Harry Scrivenor was replaced by Richard Johnson, a brother-in-law of William Crawshay who owned the Cyfarthfa Ironworks at Merthyr Tydfil. The new chairman was Robert Kennard and together they undertook important improvements to the works.

Coking ovens replaced coking in open heaps in 1849 (an uneconomic practice). Two steam locomotives were also introduced, thus reducing the reliance on horse-drawn trams. The hot blast system was adapted for use in one of the furnaces (No 2) in 1852.

Financial problems once again brought production to a halt and fresh capital had to be raised. Management was then placed in the hands of a committee consisting of Thomas Hill, Robert Wheeley and Philip Jones, a banker who represented the Herberts of Llanarth.

In the 1850s, under manager Richard Johnson, sixteen of the Company's hundreds of horses were replaced by additional steam locomotives. Also at that time some plateways mounted on stone blocks were replaced with rolled wrought iron rails on wooden sleepers.

By 1854 the railway from Newport via Pontypool had reached Blaenavon. This major development meant that the circuitous route by tramroad and the Brecknock & Abergavenny Canal via Garnddyrys could be abandoned.

Above the furnaces can be seen the remains of a row of calcining kilns in which iron ore or 'mine' was roasted to drive off the impurities such as water, carbonic acid and sulphur. Thomas Deakin's map of 1819 shows two rows of kilns in use on the site, but these still existing ones are of a later period.

One of the burning cones of the earlier kilns has survived and can be seen to the left of the later row of kilns

Breaking up the ironstone was strenuous work, yet this task was undertaken by young girls using picks and heavy hammers. They worked shifts of 12 hours (6am to 6pm), with only a short break for lunch and earned 7 shillings a week. A visitor to Blaenavon in the early years of the 19th century described how the girls wore hobnailed boots with 'toecaps that would pull the legs off some of the ploughmen!'

> *The overlooker, a Welshman named Powell showed me round... Some women were filling and wheeling barrows of ironstone: but most were engaged inside certain wooden sheds in breaking the big lumps of iron-stone... Lifting the hammer over their heads and bringing it down with manly skill and force... They were all well grown lasses, aged from 15 to 21... Mr Powell said, 'they are the finest women of this kind anywhere, and if it wasn't for the girls here I don't know what the ironworks would do.'*

Arthur Munby 1865

The raw materials of ironstone, limestone and coke were loaded into two wheel-barrows (dandies) and tipped through a hole in the side of the tunnelhead, which was a most dangerous and exhausting task for the men involved. In the early days the furnaces were open topped making this a dangerous and exhausting task. The escaping gases at night illuminated the whole area creating a most impressive sight. The more advanced furnaces enabled the gases to be collected and utilised for heating hot air stoves and steam boilers.

> *I am a 'filler'; I fill the mine, coke and limestone into the furnace; I work 12 hours and work at night every other week. I come from the County of Cork, but have been working at the iron-works for some time; I have a large family, six here and one in Ireland; I have two boys working for me here - Thomas, 10 years, old, and Timothy, 14 years old; they help in pushing the barrows called 'dandies' back and forward to the top of the furnace. Tom is rather too young to come to work, but I don't put him to do much, and I have a large family, and am obliged to put them to do something as they are able; he has not been to work long, not a year; if I had not him I should be obliged to employ a boy, which I could not afford.*

> Timothy Macarthy, aged 35

In 1709 Abraham Darby of Coalbrookdale in Shropshire discovered that coke could be used in the furnace rather than charcoal. This introduced a major saving in the cost of iron. Seven tons of charcoal were needed to make one ton of iron and seven tons of wood were needed to make one ton of charcoal. The manufacture of charcoal was a slow process and as it took something like 2,000 acres of birch coppice to support one average sized blast furnace, so suitable timber in the area was being consumed at a rapid rate.

Most historians agree that the 'take off' for the Industrial Revolution can be dated from 1760. This neatly coincides with the general adoption of coke as a fuel in the furnace rather than charcoal.

Coke is the product of heating coal to a certain temperature in the absence of air and initially the coal was coked on the flat area behind the top of the furnaces in open heaps, 70 yards in length. This uneconomic method was described by B. Faujas de Saint-Fond, following a visit to an ironworks in Scotland in 1799:

> *A quantity of coal is placed on the ground, in a round heap, of from twelve to fifteen feet in diameter, and about two feet in height. As many as possible of the large pieces are set on end, to form passages for the air; above them are thrown the smaller pieces, and coal dust, and in the midst of this circular heap is left a vacancy of a foot wide, where a few faggots are placed to kindle it. Four or five apertures of this kind are formed round the ring, particularly on the side exposed to the wind... As the fire spreads, the mass increases in bulk, becomes spongy and light, cakes into one body, and at length loses its bitumen, and emits no more smoke. It then acquires a red, uniform colour, inclining a little to white; in which state it begins to break into gaps and chinks, and to assume the appearance of the underside of a mushroom. At this moment the heap must be quickly covered with ashes to deprive it of air.*

At Blaenavon the 1849 coking ovens were built in rows on the level area above the calcining kilns (where a rugby pitch is now situated). These ovens only admitted a limited supply of air and the more inflammable ingredients of the coke were burnt away leaving practically pure carbon.

To increase the heat and make the iron molten, air was pumped into the furnace by a blowing engine to increase the heat and make the iron molten or liquid (melting point of iron 1535° C). The molten metal slowly sank down through the furnace to collect in the hearth at the bottom. The slag also became molten, but being lighter floated on top of the iron.

In the stone wall at the front of the hearth were two holes, one above the other. The top hole was called a slag notch and the bottom one the tap hole. Once every twelve hours the furnaceman equipped with a long bar would remove a clay plug and the slag would flow out to solidify and be taken away. The plug would then be replaced in the slag notch and the lower plug knocked out of the tap hole to release the liquid iron which flowed out, sparkling and bright, with the light and heat becoming more and more intense as it increased in volume.

The iron flowed from the furnace along a main channel (called a runner) in the casting house. This runner fed smaller channels at right angles (called sows) which again subdivided into shorter closed channels in which the pigs solidified. The pig beds were lined with sand and a special tool left the impression 'BLAENAVON' where the pigs formed. The whole layout in the casting house resembled a sow feeding her piglets and this gave rise to the term 'pig iron'.

The moulds for the pig iron were shaped by burying blocks of wood in the sand and when they were taken up they left a number of parallel trenches.

A special tool was used to stamp the pig moulds with the word BLAENAVON which then appeared in raised letters on the pig itself. After they had cooled the pigs were broken from the sows by the junction of each pig being given a blow with a heavy sledge hammer.

John Wilkinson pioneered the 'cupola' furnace to produce small castings. This example stands in the Blaenavon Ironworks.

Opposite the furnaces is a group of cottages (SO 250092) built between 1789 and 1792. Facing rows of cottages were constructed first to house skilled workers the ironmasters brought with them from the Midlands. This reflected in the brick arching over the doors and windows - a typical Staffordshire practice. For the time this was industrial housing of high quality. At a later date the central connecting terrace was built to provide a company office on the ground floor and dormitory accommodation for single workers on the upper floor. This central row was converted into dwellings in the 1860s.

This group of houses later became known as Stack Square, after a tall stack, erected in the central area and connected to a steam engine which supplied the blast for the furnaces. The stack was demolished in 1912 but the houses which are now unoccupied, provide an exhibition area with a model of the ironworks of special interest to visitors.

According to the 1851 Census, 84 people lived in the Square and no doubt they were all employed by the Blaenavon Ironworks Company. As many as ten people lived in one of these houses and one couple even managed to raise nineteen children in one of these dwellings, consisting of just two rooms on each floor and a larder.

The tall chimney stack which used to stand in the middle of Stack Square was in a dangerous condition by the early part of the twentieth century and it was decided to pull it down. Demolition accordingly took place one day in January 1912 and a large number of the town's inhabitants gathered at a safe distance to watch the giant brick chimney being felled.

The Company Shop

In the early days part of Stack Square was used as a Company Shop which was the earliest in Blaenavon: its first two managers were Isaac Rosser and Israel Morgans. After a while the shop was moved to premises in North Street, opposite the old Police Station.

Known as the 'Truck' or 'Tommy' shop these premises originally bene-fited the workers who were able to obtain goods on credit against advances on their wages, and many of them were on the verge of destitution when they started work.

At first the food sold was of good quality and at a reasonable price, but gradually abuses began to creep in. For instance the Company started to fix prices above those previously to be found in Abergavenny and to make trading in the Company Shop compulsory for their employees.

Prices in Blaenavon's Company Shop were raised to 25% higher than normal prices and a credit note system was used where payment for items bought by workers was deducted from their wages. This meant that very often when men called at the pay office at the end of the month, they found that they had no wages to draw, and there might even be a small debt which would be carried forward to the next month's pay.

Another problem was that payment of wages was made in the public houses where the workers were often kept waiting until the early hours of the morning and there was always a great temptation to squander their anticipated money on beer.

The 'Truck' system was hated by the workers and Blaenavon strikers in 1822 and 1830 placed it at the head of their grievances as it enabled employers to undermine any wage structure by charging excessive prices for the necessities of life.

Various governments attempted to deal with the practice but one of the problems was that very often the ironmasters were also magistrates and the Acts were ignored. In 1829 a report into the 'Paying of Workmen's Wages in Goods' stated that the practice was common in the hills of Monmouthshire and that wages were sometimes paid in ale so that other tradesmen (e.g. shoemakers) were unable to obtain payment at all.

The Anti-Truck Act (1831) was introduced by Benjamin Hall (1802-67) in an attempt to curtail the infamous truck system but it was still many years before it came to an end. The payment of wages in public houses was declared illegal in 1842.

Small coins of uniform size called 'Dibs' and stamped 'Blaenavon Shops Limited' bore the exchange value of 4d, 6d or 7d etc.

BLAENAVON SHOPS
NEAR
PONTYPOOL
MON
LIMITED

This three-storey building was the first Company Shop and was known as the 'Truck Shop'. The word comes from truckier - to barter - and in this instance the employees bartered their labour in return for provisions. Workers were paid in tokens once a month and sometimes at six week intervals. This 'long pay' was widely hated among the ironworkers and strikers at Blaenavon in October 1816 are quoted as saying that "we are prepared to return to work if we can have a weekly wage and also if we can buy goods where we please." It was many years before the system was changed.

> *Anything from a pin to a shroud could be bought at such shops and the masters instituted laws by which the workers were forced to buy there, often at prices thirty per cent higher than that of goods offered by private enterprise, which was naturally discouraged if not banned.*

Alexander Cordell 1957

The impressive water balance tower dominating the ironworks site was built in 1839 to provide a means of lifting loaded trams to a higher level

The Balance Tower

This massive tower was built by James Ashwell in 1839 for the purpose of raising single trams loaded with pig iron to the tramroad. From here the trams were pulled by horses via the Pwlldu tunnel and along Hill's tramroad to the Garnddyrys Forge (see page 64). It was a very large structure just to raise a single tram at a time, containing not more than one or two tons of pig iron. Its building cost of about £22,000 must have been very hard for Ashwell to justify.

The tower worked on the same principle as the early water balance pits. From the 1820s these were a common feature of the South Wales mining scene. The principle was simple but efficient. Two buckets, each with rails on top, were connected by a chain passing over a braked sheave set in a cast-iron frame above. A loaded tram was run onto one bucket at the bottom, and the bucket at the top, carrying an empty tram, was filled with water. It was allowed to fall, controlled by the brake, and raised the loaded tram to the top. When it was in operation local people used to refer to it as the 'guillotine,' due to the action of the cages moving past the oval openings in the tower.

This most attractive feature, dominating the ironworks site, is the most perfect example of a stone balance tower in Wales.

Plateway rails at the base of the water balance tower

Examples of later iron rails produced by the Blaenavon Company. It used to be said that the world was girdled with Blaenavon iron. The product was so famous and superior that the demand for it could not be met and three other British works entered into an agreement with the Blaenavon Company that allowed them to stamp 'Blaenavon Iron Co' on their rails. This also ensured good sales. The demand for iron rails came not only from the British railway companies but also from countries such as Russia, America, France, Belgium, Italy, Spain, Germany and Austria. But by 1870, Blaenavon had ceased to produce iron rails due to the fact that the works was not able to compete with the high quality Bessemer steel rails which by that time were being produced at Ebbw Vale.

A story is often told of an Eastern Valley man who emigrated to Australia. During a long wait on a wayside railway station he began thinking of his homeland and became quite homesick. Then looking down to the rails in front of him, he saw stamped on them, 'BLAENAVON CO.' He was so overcome with emotion that he jumped down and kissed the rails that had been made in the town of his birth.

The Blaenavon Brickworks

A constant supply of refractory bricks to line the furnaces was an essential in the smelting of iron. To provide these a main brickworks was built near the workmens' cottages known as Bunkers Row. Much of the work was undertaken by female labour.

The girls were required to tread the fireclay on a heated floor into a thick and even consistency by saturating it with water. The mixture was then moved to the brickmaking sheds where other girls were employed to mould the heavy lumps of clay into bricks. These were then fed into the kilns for firing at a temperature almost approaching to white heat. After the fire had been withdrawn the bricks were allowed to cool down slowly until it was possible for the girls to unload the kiln. This was very dirty and heavy work and they must have suffered with badly blistered hands.

In 1865 Arthur Munby visited the Blaenavon brickworks and recorded in his journal that 'ten girls, three to each kiln' and 'a shoveller' did all the work, 'with a gaffer over them.' Their ages ranged from fifteen to twenty-one and they were dressed in 'coarse smocks' and 'strong laced boots'.

Workers at the Upper Brickyard around the turn of the century

After the thrust of production at Blaenavon had moved to the other side of the Afon Lwyd, by the end of 1879 the Blaenavon Works was converted into a Limited Company, under the title of Blaenavon Company, Limited. The first Chairman was Samuel Laing, then Chairman of the London, Brighton and South Coast Railway, and a prominent figure in British commerce. In 1889 he was succeeded in the Chairmanship of the Blaenavon Company by H. J. Kennard, who with his brothers Arthur and Edward, had occupied seats on the Directorate since the formation of the Company.

H. J. Kennard died in 1896 and he was succeeded on the Board by his son R. W. Kennard who was was elected Chairman 1903. For nearly three-quarters of a century, through four generations, the Kennard family were not only closely associated with, but controlled and guided the fortunes of Blaenavon.

After 1900 the old ironworks at North Street was no longer in use and permission was given by the owners for the removal of facing stones from the furnaces for the building of St James Church. As a result of this demolition work the three bottle-shaped brick-built furnaces were exposed.

The blast furnaces in 1970 before restoration work started

This picture taken in 1911 shows a gang of workmen removing dressed stone from the front of Nos 4 & 5 furnaces. Carts and horses were loaned by the Blaenavon Company for the stone to be transported to a site at Cae White, a few hundred yards away where the new St James Church was being constructed.

In the late 1960s the National Coal Board sold the ironworks site to Blaenavon Urban District Council for land reclamation. Stack Square was declared unfit for habitation and the residents rehoused. In 1972 the Department of the Environment took the site into their care and two years later work started on consolidating the remaining buildings with the intention of turning the site into a museum. It is now under the care of Cadw: Welsh Historic Monuments, and is open to the public from Easter to the end of September. Special arrangements for party visits outside this period can be made by contacting the Tourism Section of Torfaen County Borough Council (Tel: 01633 648082)

Dominating the Ironworks car park (developed in the 1980s) is this 22 ft tall seven ton steam hammer (invented by James Nasmyth in 1839) which was originally installed at the Doncaster Works at Forgeside, Blaenavon and moved to this location in March 1987. Steam was used to operate a piston which lifted the hammer and when the pressure was released it fell by gravity. A valve controlled the amount of steam introduced, thus producing long or short strokes as required. It used to be said that a skilled operator could crack the shell of an egg with this hammer!

Doncasters had used it for some important projects which included development work on the Olympus engines which power Concorde. In addition it helped to manufacture parts for the Pegasus engine which powers the Harrier vertical take-off fighter planes. Today, the hammers at the Doncaster Works are hydraulically driven but it was on the older steam hammers that the reputation of this works was founded.

SIDNEY GILCHRIST THOMAS

Sidney Gilchrist Thomas was one of the most important figures of the Industrial Revolution, for his work led to the major growth in steel production across the world after 1878. He was born in Canonbury, London in 1850. His father, William Thomas, was a Welshman employed in the Solicitor's Department of the Inland Revenue Office. His mother, Millicent was Scottish and her maiden name was Gilchrist.

The death of his father prevented Sidney taking any form of higher education, and at the age of sixteen he became a junior clerk at Stepney magistrates court., at a salary of £90 per year. He was employed there for the next ten years, but devoted his spare time to the study of chemistry. During one of the evening classes he attended at Birbeck College, the lecturer commented that the man who could eliminate phosphorus in the Bessemer convertor would make his fortune.

Sidney immediately began to look for an answer to this problem and it soon became an obsession. He set up a small laboratory at his home and also used the laboratories at Birbeck Institute. He came to the conclusion that the answer lay in the lining of the convertor. At this time the lining was made of 'acid' bricks and the elimination of phosphorus (which was also acid) could not take place. Sidney hit upon the idea of using a non-acid lining and found that Dolomite limestone suited his purpose. He now badly needed to put this theory into practice.

In 1875 the Blaenavon Company advertised for an analytical chemist and Sidney applied for the position, but it was his cousin Percy Gilchrist who secured the position. It was not long before Sidney had persuaded his cousin to conduct some experiments in his new laboratory. They were carried out secretly, mostly at night and without the knowledge and consent of Edward Martin the works manager.

Sidney travelled up to Blaenavon by train every weekend and the two cousins made steady progress with their experiments. One evening Edward Martin, caught them at their secret work and was so impressed with the results of their experiments that he at once offered them the facilities of the Blaenavon Works for larger scale trials. In addition he undertook to purchase a share in the patent.

When the experiments were first announced they were scorned but further demonstrations in 1879, led to a flood of interest from the industrial centres of Europe and the United States. The first continental licence was granted in 1890 for £20,000 and in December of that year the American rights were sold to Andrew Carnegie for 250,000 dollars with royalties on steel made.

It was certainly an epoch-making discovery, for geologists estimated that 90% of Europe's iron ore contained more than one part of phosphorous to a thousand parts of iron and steel made from phosphoric ores too brittle for extensive use without effective lining of the furnaces.

Sidney Gilchrist Thomas 1850-85

The name of Sidney Gilchrist Thomas is more widely known abroad than in his own country and it is ironic that his achievements helped to create the German steel industry. Herr Albert, a German industrialist even had plaster casts made of Thomas to remind his fellow countrymen of 'a great benefactor.' The advent of World War I stopped a project for setting up a statue of Sidney Gilchrist Thomas in the centre of Luxemburg.

Percy Carlyle Gilchrist (1850 - 1935) in later life

Edward Pritchard Martin (1844-1910), who as Manager of the Blaenavon Company helped to progress the experiments of Sidney Gilchrist Thomas and Percy Gilchrist

These two young men, Thomas and Gilchrist of Blaenavon, did more for Britain's greatness than all the Kings and Queens put together. Moses struck the rock and brought forth water. They struck the useless phosphoric ore and transformed it into steel.

Andrew Carnegie

This discovery at Blaenavon of the process whereby phosphorous could be eliminated was a tremendous step forward and by its means phosphoric ores were brought into practical steel-making.

Britain's supplies of iron ore were limited and ironically the cousins' discovery merely served to open the doors for Andrew Carnegie in Pitsburgh USA, and Alfred Krupp of Essen, Germany to exploit their respective country's vast resources of ores having high phosphorous content.

An important by-product of the process was 'basic' or 'Thomas' slag, which is used as fertiliser.

In 1881 Sidney Gilchrist Thomas travelled to the United States as the guest of Andrew Carnegie and toured for two months. But sadly his health started to deteriorate and four years later on 1 February, 1885, just before his thirty-fifth birthday, he died in Paris from lung trouble probably induced by the use of chemicals in his experiments.

This red granite obelisk commemorating Sidney Gilchrist Thomas can be seen at the ironworks. It was originally sited in front of Coity House at Forgeside and was designed by the Newport sculptors H. Davis & Sons. The bronze head of Sidney Gilchrist Thomas was designed and cast by the sculptor Fred Mancini. This memorial was unveiled at Forgeside on July 6th 1960, before a large gathering of chairmen, directors, managers and metallurgists of large steel companies through-out Europe. The ceremony was performed by Mr G. H. Latham, President of the Newport & District Metallurgical Society and Chairman of the Whitehead Iron & Steel Company. He was assisted by Mr F. W. Cartwright, Managing Director of the Steel Company of Wales.

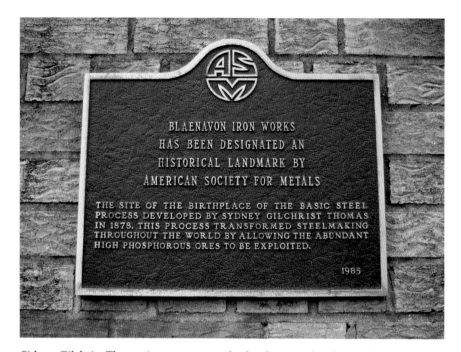

Sidney Gilchrist Thomas's memory was further honoured in September 1986 when leaders of the American Society for Metals visited Blaenavon Ironworks to dedicate the site as one of their historic landmarks. This ironworks was only the second site in Britain to receive the award. The other is the ironbridge at Telford and there are more than 40 additional ones around the world. The Society's managing director, who unveiled the plaque commented, 'It's remarkable to think all we have today came from such small beginnings and such a remarkable invention. This is truly the birthplace of modern steel processing, the technology that was developed here since the works were established in 1789 has paved the way.'

> *Before Sidney Gilchrist Thomas came to Blaenavon, not an ounce of basic steel had ever been produced; in 1973 the world's output of steel was about 700 million tons and almost all by the basic process invented by Sidney Gilchrist Thomas and his cousin between 1877 and 1878 at Blaenavon.*

> Tom Grey Davies 1975

The surviving cast houses in front of Nos 3 and 1 furnaces

Nos 4 and 5 furnaces were built in 1810 and are quite well preserved. The facing stones were removed in 1911 for use in the construction of St James Church.

Reconstruction by Michael Blackmore, depicting Blaenavon Ironworks as it would have appeared when fully operational

Son et Lumierére at Blaenavon Ironworks September 2001

Chronology of the Development and Demise
of Ironmaking at Blaenavon

1600	Iron furnace at Blaenavon - site unknown
1782	Hill & Co open Bridge Colliery
1788	Hill, Hopkins and Pratt secure lease of land at Blaenavon
1789	Blaenavon Ironworks under construction and production commenced
1790	Pig iron is being sold by the company
1796	Tramroad to canal head at Pontnewynydd is completed
179?	Death of Thomas Hopkins
179?	Death of Benjamin Pratt
1800	Three blast furnaces in operation at Blaenavon
1810	Nos 4 & 5 furnaces are put into blast
1812	Brecknock & Abergavenny Canal is completed
1815	Existing coal level extended to form the Pwll-du Tunnel
	Death of Samuel Hopkins
1817	Garnddyrys Forge sends its first iron to Newport via the B & A Canal
1824	Death of Thomas Hill
1825	Road from Abergavenny to Blaenavon is constructed
1827	Death of Thomas Hill the younger
1830	Five furnaces in operation producing 12,571 tons
1833	Blaenavon pioneers use of 'hot blast' in South Wales
1836	Thomas Hill the third sells the company to the Blaenavon Iron & Coal Company for £220,000
1839	Water Balance Tower is built by James Ashwell
1840	Three new furnaces put into blast
	The Company starts producing iron rails
	James Ashwell resigns.
1841	The Blaenavon Iron & Coal Company is employing 2,002 people (this includes 135 boys and 36 girls under the age of 13 years)
1845	Henry Scrivenor is appointed manager
1849	Coking ovens are built
1851	Census shows that 84 people are living in Stack Square
1853	The hot blast process is adopted at Blaenavon
1854	Monmouthshire Railway Co. open their line to Blaenavon
	New engine house is built at the ironworks to house new steam engine
1857	Crumlin Viaduct is completed using Blaenavon iron
1859	A new Forge and Rail Mill is opened at Forgeside on the opposite side of the valley
1860c	Forge and Mill at Garnddyrys closes
	R. W. Kennard elected Chairman of the Blaenavon Company Ltd
1861	Hill's Tramroad is abandoned
1862	John Paton is engaged as Works Manager at salary of £500 per annum
1863	1,000 tons of scrap removed from Garnddyrys
1864	Blaenavon Iron & Coal Co. is liquidated and Blaenavon Company Ltd. is formed with nominal capital of £400,000 in £50 shares

1865	Tyre Mill and Steel Works is opened at Forgeside
1868	The first furnace at Forgeside is brought into operation
	LNWR opens Blaenavon-Brynmawr line
1869	New furnace is blown in at Forgeside
1870	Blaenavon Company sells out to the Blaenavon Iron & Steel Company Ltd
	Death of R. W. Kennard
1874	E.P. Martin is appointed as General Manager
1875	Iron industry in deep depression
1876	Percy Carlyle Gilchrist is appointed works chemist at Blaenavon
	The Company is re-named Blaenavon Iron & Steel Co., Ltd.
1877	Sidney Gilchrist Thomas and Percy Carlyle Gilchrist begin experiments
	They later announce the success of their experiments in London
1878	First steel is produced at Forgeside, Blaenavon
	The Blaenavon Iron & Steel Company goes into liquidation
1880	Introduction of the Bessemer process and a mill for producing tyres is built.
1889	H. J. Kennard becomes Chairman of the Blaenavon Company Ltd
1896	Death of H. J. Kennard
1898	Steelworkers from Blaenavon are employed in Russia to set up a Bessemer plant
1903	R. W. Kennard is elected Chairman of the Company
1904	No 1 blast furnace at the old works, which had been retained to produce cold blast iron,is finally shut down
1905	Four large Bessemer convertors are built
1908	No 9 furnace is completed
1911	Blast furnaces at old works are robbed of stone to build St James Church
1912	Electric plant replaces steam power at the tyre mill
1913	New Otto ovens are started at Forgeside
1914	Shell steel is produced for the Western front, World War I
1920	New blast furnace at Forgeside provides additional output of 1,800 tons
1922	The Blaenavon Company shows a loss of £68,481
1928	The Blaenavon Company make a profit of £2,587
1929	Plant is sold to pay off Company debts
1938	Last furnace at Forgeside closes down
1939	Steel is produced at Blaenavon for the first time in 20 years, after a new works has been built with assistance from the Nuffield Trust
1949	The solid wheel and axle plant is sold to a French firm for £160,000
1957	Blaenavon Company employees receive their last pay packets
1958	The Blaenavon Co., Ltd., goes into liquidation
1960	A memorial to Gilchrist Thomas and Gilchrist is set up at Forgeside
1976	Ancient Monuments Branch of the Welsh Office takes Blaenavon Ironworks site into its guardianship
1986	Cadw announces that £300,000 will be spent on Blaenavon Ironworks
1989	The bi-centenary of Blaenavon Ironworks is celebrated
2000	The Blaenavon Industrial Landscape achieves World Heritage status

WALK ONE

Following the Iron from Blaenavon to Llanfoist

10.2km (6.5 miles)

START: Blaenavon Ironworks Car Park (SO 248092)

The inconveniences of carrying on the works, and of doing business of any kind, were very great in the old days. Commercial affairs moved along very slowly; there being no steam power, the pig iron from the furnaces was taken in the iron trams drawn by horses, up behind the Quick Building, through the big arch, and through the tunnel, round the Tumble, to Garndyrus forge...

Lewis Browning 1906

For this linear walk it is recommended that you previously position an additional vehicle at the car park just below Llanfoist Church (SO 285134), off the B4246. The purpose of this walk is to follow as near as possible the route taken by horse-drawn trams containing loads of pig iron.

It is not possible to walk through the tunnel mentioned by Lewis Browning in the above quote (featured in detail on pages 193-5), so the route crosses the ridge to Pwll-du via the Dyne Steel Incline which was built in 1850 to improve the tramroad between Pwll-du and Blaenavon.

From the Ironworks Car Park, descend the steps and turn right along the pavement. Cross the road with care and follow pavement uphill past the Ironworks. Take the next turning on the left, passing above York House and with the top of the Balance Tower now seen on the left, follow the road uphill. Then shortly turn left between rows of lock-up garages. Go over a metal stile and follow the path between fences. The playing fields on the right were once the site of the coke ovens. Pass through a gate, keep straight on and then go over a stile on the left to descend a bank, go over a stile, then on beside a playing field and through a gate. Cross the road and follow a pavement uphill to join the Blaenavon-Brynmawr Road (B4248).

Just beyond a bus shelter (on the right), cross the road and go up a tarmac lane for a short distance. Bear left at the first corner to follow a track leading between fences and through a series of gates. In due course this track becomes a pleasant green path ascending through a largely revegetated and attractive industrial landscape.

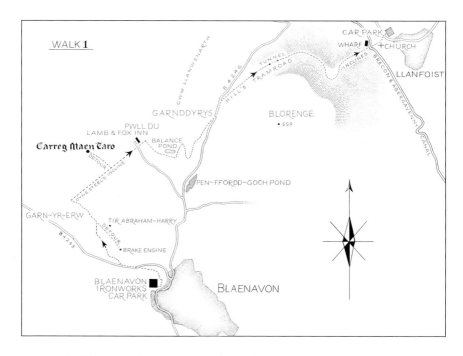

The Blaenavon landscape was the product of the human creativity of many individuals, entrepreneurs, technologists, engineers and workers, over several generations. It is an outstanding example of characteristic forms of human settlement and the exploitation of mineral and energy resources associated with the coal and iron industries in the first phases of the Industrial Revolution.

World Heritage Industrial Landscape
Nomination Document 2000

Mineral working in the early days was often a part-time activity carried on by local farmers, but by the early 19th century the Blaenavon Company had monopolised the mineral take with numerous levels being driven into the hillsides with ever deeper shafts following in the 1840s.

But by the mid 19th century, the sources of ironstone had become unprofitable to work and the Blaenavon furnaces were then fed with imported ores from Spain.

Ahead will be seen a stone stack, (SO 239102) marking the site of Hill Pits, which, situated at an altitude of 432m (1,420 feet) above sea level, were sunk during the late 1830s by the Blaenavon Iron & Coal Company to provide ironstone and coal for the Blaenavon Ironworks. Coal was also mined here for selling to external markets to help improve the Company's financial situation during slumps in the iron trade. The pit was connected to Blaenavon Ironworks by a horse-worked tramroad and inclined plane. It was in operation for about 56 years, ceasing production in 1894.

The stone chimney stack (SO 239102) is built of blocks of dressed stone. Perfectly square and standing 6 metres high, it once served a boiler house that powered a steam winding engine for the twin shafts of Hill Pits which were filled in May 1963.

A short detour to see an interesting relic

Follow the old tramroad to the right, shortly passing on the left a path leading up to the ruins of Ty Abraham Harry.

Ty Abraham Harry (SO 240102) is a ruined farmhouse perched on the hillside to the east of Hill Pits. It is said to be named after its original occupant who mined coal here long before the days of tramroads. In 1936 the building was occupied by William Llewellyn and his wife Elizabeth who were then both aged 85. William had farmed here for at least sixty years and until his retirement had worked underground as well. He was able to claim that he had worked in every colliery in Blaenavon, including Hill Pits.

Follow the tramroad to the top of a short incline. On the left can be seen the remains of the braking system (SO 243099) which controlled the descent of the trams. (The inclined plane is shown on maps from 1844 but it went out of use by 1888). This ingenious braking device was well engineered and constructed of wrought and cast iron. It was excavated in 1979.

> *The brake engine is not marked on the 1844 tithe map but it must have been present or constructed very soon afterwards. In 1880 a small building stood to the rear of it and it has been suggested that this was a stable for the horses used in shunting trams at the top of the incline. The brake engine may have been made within the Blaenavon Company and, considering its relatively simple task, is a sophisticated piece of engineering.*

John van Laun, 'Hill Pits, Blaenavon',
Industrial Archaeology Review 3 (1979)

The remains of a wrought iron band brake set in a pit at the bottom of an incline plane above Garn-yr-erw. Its purpose was to control the rate of descent of the trams.

Return along the tramroad to Hill Pits and continue along the track to pass a pool with a small concrete dam. Just beyond here turn right to ascend an incline leading up to the ridge above. The lower part of it is generally waterlogged in places, but the ground improves as you get higher.

This incline (Dyne Steel's) is half a mile long and consisted of four lines of rails. An engine with four wire ropes to haul the trams was mounted on the ridge. The system worked as follows: One truck was ready loaded at the bottom. Two trucks were on the summit (one full and one empty) and the truck at the Pwll-du side of the ridge was empty. In this position, and at the sound of a bell signal the engine would be set in motion and all four trucks would start moving at the same time. They were loaded at the Garn-yr-erw side and unloaded at Pwll-du.

On the skyline you will pass through a cutting to reach the crest of the ridge. From here extensive views across to the Brecon Beacons, the Black Mountains and the summit of the Blorenge may be enjoyed.

Near the top of the incline can be seen a semi-circular pond about 80m long and 30m wide (SO 244108). A lake running from it towards the top of the incline may have carried water which was used for raising steam in boilers to power the winding engine.

Another Short Detour

Go left along the ridge track to reach Carreg Maen Taro (SO 238113), a roughly hewn stone which according to local tradition is said to mark the site of an ancient battle. It is however more likely to be a boundary stone and stands 1.7m high at the border of the Blaenavon, Llanfoist Fawr and Llanelly parishes.

Carreg Maen Taro, on the ridge above Pwll-du has the letters 'B' and 'M' carved on two of its faces - 'B' for Breconshire and 'M' for Monmouthshire. This stone also served as an important marker showing the limit of the Blaenavon Ironworks lease.

Return to the top of Dyne Steel's Incline and head down the Pwll-du side towards a white building situated directly below. This is the Lamb and Fox Inn, which has a unique atmosphere and is popular with walkers and cavers. This is one of the highest pubs in Wales and from the lounge window is an impressive view over the Usk Valley.

Follow a track to the right of the inn beside a stone wall, heading towards the Blorenge aerials, which can be seen on the skyline. Pass above a rather boggy area and then head across to the site of an old Balance Pond. This rectangular stone lined hollow once held water used to operate a lifting system in the Pwll-du quarry (SO 251115) directly below this point.

On the hillside directly above Pwll-du Quarry is the old Balance Pond which was constructed to supply water used to operate a water balance (see page 39 for the operation of the Blaenavon Water Balance Tower). By these means trams loaded with limestone were raised from the quarry floor.This picture was taken immediately after heavy rain and it shows the rectangular stone-lined hollow full of water, but it is normally dry, having been drained many years ago.

Walk along the edge of the pond to the far end and then follow a track down past a hollow and around heaps of stones, to make a diagonal descent to Hill's Tramroad. A short detour to the left provides a good view of Pwll-du Quarry.

Pwll-du Quarry was established at the head of Cwm Llanwenarth in the first decades of the nineteenth century to provide limestone for the newly erected furnaces at Blaenavon. Masonry can be seen at the top of a balance shaft which was cut vertically down through the quarry, for the purpose of raising tramloads of limestone to the level of the upper tramroad. The hoist was operated by a counter-balance system similar to the one used in the Balance Tower at Blaenavon Ironworks. Trams entered the bottom of the shaft from the quarry floor through an opening which at the present time is partially blocked and difficult to enter. A map of 1814 indicates that the quarry was being worked at that time but according to the 1880 Ordnance Survey Map it would appear that by then it was no longer in use.

Hill's Tramroad named after the Ironmaster Thomas Hill provides an ideal walking route around the head of Cwm Llanwenarth to the site of the Garnddyrys Forge.

Retrace your steps along Hill's Tramroad and follow it around above Cwm Llanwenarth. Take care not to walk too close to the edge of the track for there is a steep drop below. Pause, to look across the valley at the site of Garnddyrys Forge and the ruins of workers' cottages. In the distance can be seen the shapely Skirrid Fawr while on the other side of the Usk Valley is the distinctive cone of Mynydd Pen y Fal, popularly known as the Sugar Loaf.

On reaching the head of the narrow valley, cross a diagonal track which is an old parish road known as Rhiw Ifor. Then scramble across the stream where the old bridge which once supported the tramroad has disintegrated. Walk on past the ruins of a little stone building which once served as a blacksmith's forge providing an emergency shoeing service for the horses pulling the trams.

If you look back from here you will be able to pick out a convergence of tracks on the other side of Cwm Llanwenarth. The main tramroad curves around to the top of the Pwll-du Quarry, while a lower track, which is now poorly defined, leads to the foot of the quarry. Cutting diagonally down the hillside is the prominent path of Rhiw Ifor which is the original route down to Govilon.

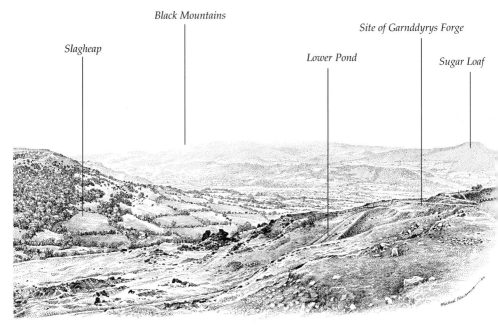

Black Mountains

Slagheap

Site of Garnddyrys Forge

Lower Pond

Sugar Loaf

The site of Garnddyrys Forge above Cwm Llanwenarth

The next section of the tramroad is not very obvious for it is hidden beneath a pile of boulders and earth which have slipped from the hillside above. But a narrow path is easily followed and ahead now can seen a strange looking mound of dark material. This is a heap of slag which has been shaped by over a century of wind and rain. But sadly its 'head' has fallen off in recent years with the result that it no longer resembles a prehistoric monster.

Leave the track which heads down past the pile of slag and walk across to a level strip of land which was the site of the Garnddyrys Forge and Rolling Mill. (Route continued on Page 78)

Iron accommodates itself to all our wants, our desires, and even our caprices: it is equally serviceable to the arts, the sciences, to agriculture, and war; the same ore furnishes the sword, the ploughshare, the spring of a watch or of a carriage, the chisel, the chain, the anchor, the compass, the cannon, and the bomb. It is a medicine of much virtue, and the only metal friendly to the human frame.

Dr Ure 1841

The Garnddyrys Forge and Rolling Mill

The mountain was shuddering to the forge-hammers of Garndyrus, and faintly on the wind came the plaintive singing of the Irish hauliers. Llanfoist farms were sleeping in the pit-blackness below, their blind windows winking at the stars, and Abergavenny was a town of dead, strangled by the ribbon of the Usk that gleamed and flashed in the scudding moonlight.

Alexander Cordell
Rape of the Fair Country 1959

View from Pwll-du Quarry towards the site of Garnddyrys Forge and Rolling Mill

It was Alexander Cordell who first awakened interest in Garnddyrys when his famous novel *Rape of the Fair Country* was published in 1959. Industrial archaeology was not in vogue at that time but he undoubtedly provided inspiration for members of the Abergavenny Steam Society, who investigated this site in 1971-3. Cordell, in his novel, described Garnddyrys as an ironworks, with blast furnaces, but his interpretation was incorrect and the site was limited to producing wrought-iron bars, rails and plates.

Situated at an altitude of 400 metres (1,300 feet), Garnddyrys must have been a wild and windy place to work, especially in mid winter. It may seem a most unlikely location for an industrial undertaking, but was chosen for sound reasons. The junction between the Monmouthshire and Brecknock & Abergavenny Canals was made in 1812, and ironmasters began to direct their attention to forming links with the B & A. The reason is not far to seek. The B & A Act contained a clause which stipulated that goods originating on the B & A would be carried through to Newport by the Monmouthshire at B & A rates, which in March 1817, the company were considering lowering from 3d to 2d per ton/mile on iron. This was instigated by Joseph and Crawshay Bailey of Nantyglo who were the principal freighters on the B & A. A tramroad from furnaces to forge could easily be extended to the canal at Llanfoist to take advantage of the lower tolls on the B & A. Yet another attraction lay in the Llanvihangel Tramroad, opened in 1814 from Llanfoist to Abergavenny and beyond into Herefordshire, which offered new markets for coal and for the lime burnt in the Llanfoist kilns as well as iron refined at an intermediate point.

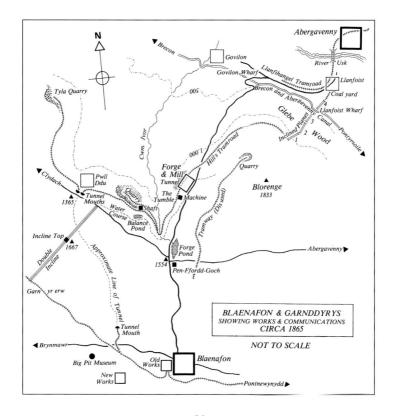

BLAENAFON & GARNDDYRYS
SHOWING WORKS & COMMUNICATIONS
CIRCA 1865

NOT TO SCALE

Site Features

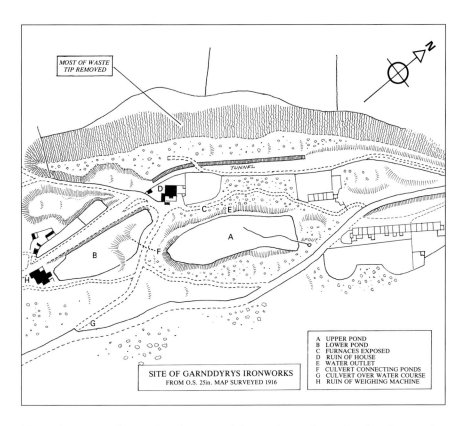

MOST OF WASTE
TIP REMOVED

TUNNEL

D

C E

A

SPOUT

B

F

H

G

SITE OF GARNDDYRYS IRONWORKS
FROM O.S. 25in. MAP SURVEYED 1916

A UPPER POND
B LOWER POND
C FURNACES EXPOSED
D RUIN OF HOUSE
E WATER OUTLET
F CULVERT CONNECTING PONDS
G CULVERT OVER WATER COURSE
H RUIN OF WEIGHING MACHINE

The main tramroad passed to the west of the works at a lower level and entered a short cut and cover tunnel (SO 259118) which is a Scheduled Ancient Monument. It was constructed to protect the tramroad from the large quantities of slag produced by the forge. It is about 2.0m high, 2.2m wide and the total length is about 135m. There is a section of about 35m which with care can be entered through a hole in the side wall. Two subsidiary tunnels strike off at right angles from the main tunnel towards the forge area. One of the tunnels is 6m in length, 1m high and 0.75m wide.

At the southern end of the site beside the tramroad can be seen the remains of a 'Weigh-house' as indicated on the 1819 map. Here the quantities of pig iron and coal brought to the works were recorded.

Above the forge site were two ponds (now usually dry), each approximately one acre in area. Water was conveyed from the upper pond to the lower by means of a stone lined underground culvert. The upper pond probably supplied water to boilers for a steam engine which was installed before 1833. This would have driven the rolling mills. A lake (shown as 'watercourse to Garnddyrys' on the 1819 map) which served the ponds can be seen running from the balance pond and curving past the head of Cwm Llanwenarth towards Garnddyrys. Around 100m from the forge its course is indeterminable.

This outlet which can be seen in the retaining wall of the upper pond was a supply point to the work- ings below. A sale notice dated 1833 mentions a steam engine on the site which provided power for the forge and rolling mill.

It took 1.5 tons of pig iron to make 1 ton of wrought iron and prior to 1840 the output of wrought iron was only about 78 tons per week, but following improvements on the site this went up to 200 tons and by 1841 had risen to 300 tons per week.

The fuel used at the forge was traditionally charcoal, but in 1784 Henry Cort patented a reverberatory furnace which allowed raw coal to be used to burn out carbon. By keeping the fuel separate from the iron contamination with sulphur was prevented. This 'puddling process' took place in a 10ft by 5ft furnace. At one end was the fire and at the flue end was the bowl where pig iron was laid. The two were separated by the fire bridge so that the heat could play down on the iron bringing it to a semi-molten state. The puddler manipulated the bloom and controlled the draught by a damper in the chimney until after about two hours the iron had 'come to nature'. It was then withdrawn and taken to the hammer to be consolidated.

To be a puddler required immense strength not only to 'rabble' the semi-molten iron in the furnace but also lift the 2cwt bloom or 'ball' to be hammered. Puddlers therefore became the aristocrats of the iron industry; they were natty dressers and considered a 'good catch'. However, their hard life took its toll, the heat caused them to drink large quantities of beer and they often went blind at an early age.

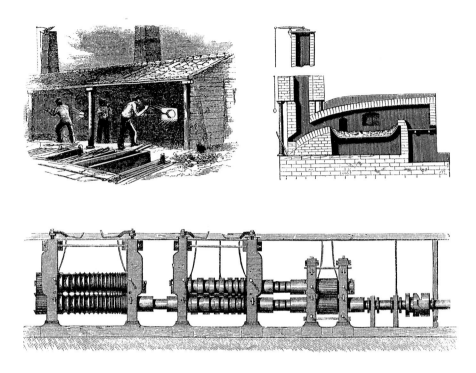

Illustrations from *'Tomlinson's Encyclopedia of Useful Arts'* c.1851.

In the mill furnace the 'blooms' were reheated and taken to the rolls. Cort had also patented the grooved roll. which rather like a mangle, rolled wrought iron into bars or rods of almost any profile. A pair of cast-iron rolls, grooved according to the shape required, were mounted in bearings within a robust iron housing. Screws set outside the housing enabled the pressure on the heated iron to be adjusted. The rolls were mechanically powered (mostly by steam engines) and as the length of pre-heated iron passed between them it was pressed or 'rolled' into the desired cross section. It usually required several passes through the rollers to obtain the required shape. Thomas Cooke employed by John Hanbury of Pontypool is credited with inventing the rolling mill in about 1720, but it was Henry Cort who introduced grooved rolls in 1784.

The 'Monster' slag heap at Garnddyrys photographed by the author in 1985 has now unfortunately lost its 'head' which was removed by vandals in recent years.

This how Garnddyrys may have looked in about 1850. Billowing smoke rises from the tall chimneys of the puddling furnaces where pig iron was converted into wrought iron. A nearby rolling mill produced the final products such as bars, rails and plates. Operations here came to an end by 1860, when the plants was dismantled and the rolling mill incorporated into a new works erected on the Coity side of Blaenavon at Forgeside.

73

Site of the Garnddyrys Forge and Rolling Mill

This cut and cover tunnel was constructed to protect the tramroad from the large quantities of slag produced by the forge

Workers' Housing

This was once a thriving community, a little town of people who lived their lives on the edge of a golden valley, who laughed and cried and brought forth children; who made iron of a quality incomparable.

Alexander Cordell 1957

The 1851 census tells us that about three hundred people lived in the vicinity of the Garnddyrys Forge. They were mainly Welsh but some came from Staffordshire and Ireland. Many of the men would have worked as puddlers, shingler, rollers and hauliers whilst the women and children were employed on less skilled tasks.

Pwll-du Howard was once the residence of the Garnddyrys Overman and it is is said that the hillside above is known as 'The Tumble', in memory of an incident when a certain Dic Shon tumbled down the steep slope and broke his leg.

The cottages where the Garnddyrys workers lived were very conveniently situated and the nearest dwellings to the Forge site were in the Garnddyrys Square. This consisted of twenty houses built on three sides of a rectangle, providing 5,10 and 5 houses on the respective sides. By 1870 these cottages had been partly demolished and the site is now only marked by piles of scattered stones. Garnddyrys Row consisted of 15 houses in one block. They are clearly shown on the 1828 OS map and were abandoned before 1938. Families living at Garnddyrys were largely Welsh but many came from Staffordshire and Ireland.

The remains of a cottage known as Pwll-du Howard, photographed by the author in 1999

The Closure of Garnddyrys

On 22 April 1853 a shareholders' meeting was held to decide the future of Garnddyrys. It was decided to close the site and transfer the rolling mill to the new works being erected on the Coity side of Blaenavon. Appropriately this became known as Forgeside. The following extract is from the Company minutes book:-

The works having now returned to a profitable condition the Directors have again seriously considered the best means of increasing the production of wrought iron, and at the same time of still further diminishing the expense of its manufacture. They are satisfied that this may be accomplished by the removal of the mill from Garnddyrys and its re-erection, with increased power and efficiency, on the Freehold Property of the Company at Blaenavon, and they desire to call the attention of the shareholders to their reasons for this conviction.

The site of the mill at Garnddyrys has been a constant source of inconvenience and expense on account of its distance from the H.Q. at Blaenavon, and now that the Monmouthshire Canal Company have reduced their tonnages and improved the mode of conveyance along their road, these advantages are the most strikingly felt; the transit from Garnddyrys being a circuitous and expensive route of twenty four miles, while the port of Newport will be reached by a locomotive railway from Blaenavon of only 16 miles.

The power of the present mill is scarcely equal to the production of 200 tons per week. It is proposed to make the new one, eventually, more than double that power, say equal to 500 tons per week, this increase, while tending to reduce the cost of the common charges upon each ton made, will enable the company to enter more largely into the manufacture of rails and to add that of 'Tyre Iron' and 'Boiler Plates' two articles for which the Blaenafon Iron is believed to be particularly well adapted.

Taking all these points into consideration the Directors have commenced this important alteration, as the means not only of increasing very materially the profit of the concern in favourable times, but what is of equally essential importance, of saving the Company from losses in unfavourable years.

In 1860 the plant was dismantled and the rolling mill transferred to Forgeside, thus ending nearly half a century of operation at Garnddyrys.

Continuation of Walk One

Head up to the Blaenavon Road and follow it down for about 200 metres and then cross it to continue along Hill's Tramroad.

On the left is the site of the Garnddyrys Inn where Billy Harris was landlord during the main years of the operation of the Forge. A story is often told of a later time when a lively party took place here on the evening of Saturday 4th August 1946. At 10.15pm there was a loud creak and the floor suddenly gave way causing thirty customers to fall into the cellar. The inn was owned at this time by Facey's Brewery Co. of Abergavenny and the landlord was Mr F. Lewis.

The old Queen Victoria Inn at Garnddyrys was demolished in about 1970

In due course you will reach a shallow cutting leading to a tunnel. Adventurous walkers may choose to scramble down into it and tramp through the gloom and sheep droppings to emerge into daylight at the far end. If this subterranean route does not appeal to you then follow the path over the top continuing to enjoy the panoramic view over the Usk Valley to the Black Mountains.

Hill's Tramroad just beyond the site of the Garnddyrys Inn with Skirrid Fawr, also known as the Holy Mountain in the distance

This 'cut and cover' tunnel (SO 272129) on Hill's Tramroad was constructed in about 1821 and probably served to protect the tramroad from ground slippage. It is 50m long, 2.2m wide and 2.0m high from the original floor level.

Hill's Tramroad on the north side of the Blorenge near the top of the Llanfoist Inclines. This early transport route provides enjoyable walking and is of important historical significance as it embodies many kinds of engineering features - tran-shipment points, inclines, cuttings, embankments, tunnels and a water balance.

On rounding a corner in the hollow on the north side of the Blorenge you will see a retaining wall on the right. It was at this point that the first section of incline descended down the steep slope on the left into Cwm Craf and near here a brake engine was situated to control the descending trams. This first incline is now difficult to see and it is not a right of way, **so continue along the track beside a fence and then follow a path down to a stile. From here head straight down towards the wood and descend to the next stage of the incline.**

Go over a stile and then down to a platform where you will see a small brick hut. From here the next incline which is known as 'The Big Drop' descends steeply. A brake wheel set in a pit controlled the descent of the trams down each section of incline. Passing around the brake wheel was a continuous chain which was fastened to the trams on each line of rails. Grooves cut by the passage of the chain may be observed on certain stones still in place on the incline.

Full trams descended under gravity pulling empty ones up on the other side and no doubt accidents frequently occurred.

Looking down 'the Big Drop' - third section of the Llanfoist Incline

At the bottom of the incline go over a stile and walk on to enter a tunnel which passes under the old Wharfmaster's House and the canal. The gurgling stream which flows down the channel on the right is known as the 'Devil's Gully.' **To obtain a good view of Llanfoist Wharf, on emerging from the tunnel, ascend the steps on the left to reach the canal towpath.** In front of you now is the old Wharfemaster's House and Hill's Warehouse which today are respectively known as Boathouse Cottage and The Boathouse. This was once a very busy wharf where trams from Garnddyrys were unloaded and the iron products transferred to the waiting narrow boats to be taken on a two day journey to Newport Docks. Limestone and coal was also taken by narrow boat in the other direction to Brecon.

Return down the steps and follow the lane past Llanfoist Church to your finishing point at the car park just below the B4246.

BLAENAVON TOWN

The town of Blaenavon is situated on the south western slope of the Blorenge Mountain, at the bottom of which is the river called Afon Lwyd. From the river, which is here 1,000 feet above sea level, the town stretches up the slope, the highest point being over 12,00 feet.

Sir Joseph Bradney 1906

Blaenavon as a place name was first mentioned in the Llanover records of 1501 and the name is then more frequently in evidence towards the end of the sixteenth century. It was during the period from 1780 to 1800 that this small farming community developed into an industrial village with a thousand inhabitants.

Until 1825 Blaenavon was the leading iron town in Monmouthshire and then its importance was overtaken, first by Nantyglo and then by Ebbw Vale. Fifty years of rapid growth between 1841 and 1891 saw the town's population rise to nearly 12,000 and by 1919 it had peaked at about 13,000. Blaenavon's decline in industrial importance resulted in unemployment and migration of the population, bringing the figure down to 7,182 by 1971 and at the present time it is about 6,000. Efforts are now being made to revive the town's fortunes by the sympathetic exploitation of the area's unique industrial heritage.

Ty Mawr

This impressive mansion in Church Road was built by Samuel Hopkins in about 1800. In his time it was also known as 'Blaenavon House' to distinguish it from his second home in Nevill Street, Abergavenny, where he often stayed when he wished to indulge in the social life and milder climate of that town. He bequeathed that property to Dr Steel, the Company Surgeon and the strength of their friendship is confirmed by the fact that the doctor's first son was christened Samuel Hopkins Steel.

Ty Mawr in later years was used by subsequent directors of the Blaenavon Company as their official residence and shooting parties were also accommodated there. These visiting wealthy sportsmen enjoyed their pastime on the Blorenge and Coity Mountain grouse moors.

In 1925 the Blaenavon Company decided that they no longer needed Ty Mawr and it was leased to the local Medical Society who adapted the premises to provide hospital facilities for seventeen in-patients. There was also an out-patient department and several examination and treatment rooms.

Ty Mawr in Church Road was built by Samuel Hopkins in 1800 and was later used by directors of the Blaenavon Company as their official residence. It is now a private nursing home called 'The Beeches'.

This stone in the grounds of Ty Mawr marks the date when the mansion was enlarged by the Kennards to accommodate a greater number of guests

The Blaenavon Medical Scheme in later years became so highly regarded that it was one of the examples which provided inspiration to Aneurin Bevan in the creation of the National Health Service. In return for a small weekly contribution from employees and workers the local residents could enjoy a free medical service. Responsibility for the hospital was taken over in 1950 by the Ministry of Health as a result of the 1948 Act.

A new health centre was opened in Blaenavon in July 1980, at a cost of £130,000 and it was designed to combine the functions of a local hospital and a health centre, thus bringing together all aspects of health under one roof. During the following year, the old hospital was put up for sale by the Gwent Health Authority at a price of £30,000 and it is now a private nursing home known as 'The Beeches'. It is unfortunate that recent works have done nothing to enhance the character of this rather fine building.

In the grounds of Ty Mawr can be seen two stones inscribed 'Billy' and 'Bones' commemorating two gun dogs once owned by the Kennard family

In a subsequent excursion to Blaenavon which I made from Pontypool, I received great marks of hospitality and attention from Mr Hopkins, one of the proprietors, who is constructing a comfortable and elegant mansion at the northern extremity of this beautiful vale.

William Coxe 1801

Park House which is situated a short distance from Ty Mawr was the impressive home of three generations of the Hill family

St Peter's School

St Peter's School was built in 1816 by Sarah Hopkins in memory of her brother Samuel. They had previously opened a school on Bunker's Hill and employed a workman's wife to teach the little children of the neighbourhood. The running costs were covered by pupils paying a fee of two pence per week. As the population increased the need for a better school grew accordingly. When Samuel Hopkins died in 1815, his sister Sarah resolved to build and endow a school as a memorial to him. In doing so she made history, for this was the first purpose built school in Wales to be established by an industrial employer for the benefit of the workers' children.

The Hill family were staunch Anglicans and the school operated on the National School Society system instituted in 1811. Under the supervision of the schoolmaster, or mistress, older children taught younger pupils, in a system known as mutual instruction.

The first scholars at the school were taught to write on sand, but they soon became fine penmen and one pupil was said to be able to write the Lord's Prayer in the space of a sixpence!

The lower of three buildings which made up the school is the original and it was opened in 1816 to take 120 pupils. A tablet over the entrance, inscribed in Latin, reads:-

UT
Exore
Parvulorum
Laudes Domini
Perpetuas evocaret,
Nec non ut Fratris desideratissimi
Optimeque de se promerentis
Benevolentiae in Glenavonienses suos
Aliqua ex parte vel mortui satisfaceret,
Hunc Ludum Literarum
Suis sumtibus aedificandum curavit

SARAH HOPKINS
Anno Domini MDCCCXVI

This translates as follows:-

In order that from the mouth of children she might call forth the perpetual praises of the Lord, and that she might in some part discharge, and in the best way of deserving him, the generosity of her most dear brother, though deceased, towards his own people of Blaenavon, SARAH HOPKINS caused this school to be erected at her own expense A.D. 1816

The description of the residents of Blaenavon as Glenavonians was not an error but a 'Latinisation' of the original Welsh name, Glynavon (Glynafon), being the locality in which the ironworks were built.

James Coldwell was the first teacher and, when he was appointed House Agent to the Blaenavon Company, he was succeeded as school-master by Messrs Bachelor (twice) and Hodgson. By 1849 it became necessary to erect a second building to accommodate the infants. By now the total number of pupils had nearly trebled. This was not surprising for during the same period the population of the town had risen from 2,000 to 7,500.

Over the entrance to St Peter's School is a tablet inscribed in Latin commemorating its erection by Sarah Hopkins in 1816

St Peter's was the earliest ironworks school in Wales and originally consisted of two large rooms - one for boys and one for girls. The adjacent Infants' school was added in 1849 and the building above was built in 1860 as a purpose built Boys' School – after which the original building became the girls' school.

In the first half of the nineteenth century the school established by Sarah Hopkins was the only means of education available for the children of Blaenavon. Although the schools were called 'Blaenavon Endowed Schools' and sometimes 'Free Schools' a nominal charge for upkeep was deducted from the workmen's wages in 1856 which caused considerable friction between the proprietors and the employees, since the majority of the latter were Dissenters.

By 1860 three separate schools had been completed and a commemoration service was held in St Peter's Church with the sermon given by the Reverend Henry Thomas Hill, grandson of Thomas Hill. The *Free Press* reported;

> *The sermon was able and pathetic ... we observed several strong men convulsively sobbing ... The scholars, to the number of 500, afterwards formed a procession and marched to the residence of the respected manager of the works where they were treated to an ample supply of tea and cakes.*

The first certified teacher was Mr T. Abraham, followed in 1862 by Mr John Thomas, who afterwards became Clerk to the Council. His son Mr. I. G. Thomas followed him as Clerk.

Lewis Browning, a Blaenavon man writing in 1906 recalled his childhood and schooldays:

> *I was born in No. 4 Bunker's Hill, Blaenavon, on the 24th July, 1828, and was baptised on July 24th, 1831, when 3 years old. At that time my parents moved to Greenland Row, because it was nearer the work. It was then that I commenced going to school in the little Quick Building. In my childhood days, so my mother used to say, I was most anxious to be able to do what the older ones did, - jumping and skipping along, and being most sharp at my lessons, I was removed from Mrs Jeremiah's school much sooner than other children to the Free School, where I continued to learn more and more, so that I became quite a favourite at home, and my master (Mr John Coldwell), and also with the old lady (Miss Hopkins), and I received the highest prizes at school. Miss Hopkins's prizes were always in clothing, and my mother must have been proud of me, for circumstances were not of the best, as the family was a large one. Two of my younger brothers had to go and work underground while I was kept in school.*

In August 1959 Miss May Lewis retired as head teacher of Blaenavon Endowed Girls School. She had been head teacher for 33 years and during that time over 1,200 girls had passed under her supervision. The grand-children of some of those first girls were now pupils at the school. Following her retirement it ceased to be one of the few girls' schools in the County and was combined with the boy's school under the headship of Frank Hatherall. May Lewis had also been a member of Blaenavon UDC since 1934 and was the oldest member of the Council. She had been Chairman and was also the first woman to serve on the Council.

The last meeting of Blaenavon Church Endowed Schools was held in September 1965. From then the schools' management was conducted from the offices of the Eastern Valley Group of managers of Endowed Schools. St Peter's School closed in 1982 and, in spite of being a listed Grade II build-ing has fallen into dereliction.

It is planned to restore the original school building to its former glory as a World Heritage Centre, provide archive and learning facilities, with Heritage Lottery Fund support.

St Peter's Church

St Peter's Church was built in 1804 by Thomas Hill and Samuel Hopkins at their own expense. It was constructed in local stone and opened the following year, which was marked a great victory at Trafalgar.

Before the new church could be dedicated, an Act of Parliament had to be obtained. The preamble stated: '... *whereas a small chapel called Capel Newydd is not sufficient to contain the inhabitants desirous of attending divine service therein ... Thomas Hill and Samuel Hopkins ... Ironmasters ... have lately at their own cost and charges erected a new church at Blaenavon and have also set apart ... land as a cemetery and have faced the same with a wall.*' The Act stipulated that the wardens of the church had to be: '*Two persons, being inhabitants of the said hamlet or District of Blaenavon (not being of the people commonly called Quakers).*'

At first St Peter's Church was just a rectangular hall used as a meeting place but in time a three-sided wooden gallery was added and a western tower with six bells. However, it was many years before the chancel was built.

Thomas Hill was so pleased with the appearance of the church that he also financed the building of a Parish Church at Lye on the border of his home county of Staffordshire. It was constructed on similar lines except that it was built in brick: later additions included a taller spire and two transepts.

The first vicar of St Peter's was the Rev James Jenkins. His regnum lasted from 1805 until his resignation thirty seven years later, when he became rector of Llanfoist, near Abergavenny. He was succeeded at St Peter's by the Rev John Jones who resided in the town's first vicarage near Glantorfaen Terrace until his death at the age of seventy five.

John Jones conducted services at St Peter's at 11.00 am and 6.00 pm in English and in-between he was preaching in Welsh at Capel Newydd at 3.00 pm. An earlier service was also held at Capel Newydd at 9.00 am after which many of the chapel folk then went to St Peter's church to hear the popular John Jones preach.

When Samuel Hopkins died in 1815, he was buried in the churchyard and was followed by Thomas Hill in 1827 at the age of 59.

In 1867 the Directors of the Blaenavon Company were asked to be patrons of the church and to assist in providing an organ. They also paid for new gas lighting which enabled people sitting at the inner end of the pews to read services, whereas before they had to try and manage with the feeble light of candles.

The church yard was enlarged in 1882 at the expense of the Blaenavon Company, by whom the land was enclosed and a further extension was made in 1891, by courtesy of the Company. They agreed to maintain the boundary wall and the fabric of the church, to provide the surplices and the bread and wine for the Sacrement; they also agreed to find the rent for a glebe farm for the incumbent.

The galleries round three sides of the nave erected in 1880 to increase the seating capacity to 400, are unique for an Anglican church and give it the appearance of a Baptist Church. The galleries are supported by iron pillars which are topped with beautifully decorated ironwork

Inside the church can be seen a cast iron font which consists of a circular bowl mounted on a slender stem and bears the date 1805 when the church was consecrated.

The first person to be baptised in St Peter's was John Osland, who in later years was a collier, and lived in North Street, above the old Company Shop and subsequently in the house where the land agent's office is.

Lewis Browning 1906

A special feature of this church that is always of interest to visitors is the amount of iron used in its construction. Not only were the window frames made of iron, but also the door sills, tomb covers and even the font. The main gates are also unusual being supported by two cannon pillars with cannon ball tops. It may be assumed that left-over cannon moulds at the ironworks were used to cast these pillars.

The memorial stones in the graveyard indicate many Worcestershire and Staffordshire origins and of particular interest on the south side of the church is a group of five tombs that have cast iron covers. They include the graves of Thomas Deakin, surveyor to the Blaenavon Ironworks Company, and that of Samuel Hopkins, joint proprietor of the works. The lid of the latter tomb has simple decorated edging and its inscription plaque is now inside the church.

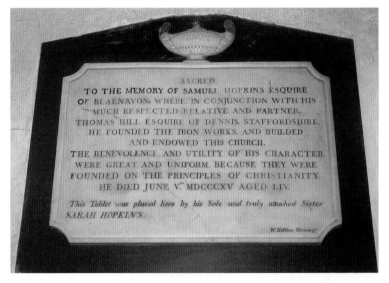

'Sacred to the memory of Samuel Hopkins, Esquire of Blaenavon, who in conjunction with his much respected relative and partner Thomas Hopkins Esquire, of Dennis, Staffordshire. He founded the ironworks and endowed this church. The benevolence and utility of his character were great and uniform, because they were founded on the principles of Christianity.
He died June Vth, MDCCCXV.

This tablet was placed here by his sole and truly attached sister SARAH HOPKINS. '

Thomas Hill is commemorated on another tablet:

'In a vault adjoining this church are deposited in the hopes
of a joyful resurrection the remains of Thomas Hill, Esq.
of Blaenavon. The kind and affectionate father of five
children,who survive to lament their severe loss and by
whom this tablet is erected to his revered memory.
He died Nov 29th, 1827, Aged 59.'

Another interesting tablet commemorates Samuel Elmes Steel MD who
was one of the town's best loved doctors. In July 1897, he had been called
to see a patient during the night of July 29th. On his return to Abergavenny,
he accidently fell from his horse and died within a few hours. He was
buried in Llanfoist Churchyard and the following year a tablet in his
memory was erected by Mr W. Burgoyne, builder and sculptor, at St.
Peter's Church, Blaenavon.

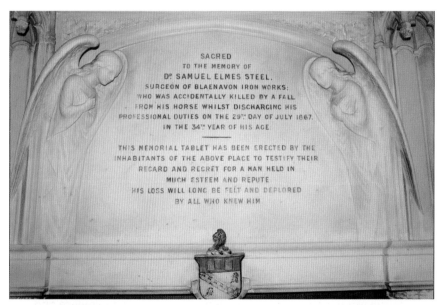

The Steel family had provided the first medical men in Blaenavon and
Drs Thomas, William and Christopher Steel, living in Abergavenny, used to
visit Blaenavon three times a week and more often in cases of emergency.
These visits continued for a number of years and their surgery was just
below the Company stables. Medicines such as salts, senna, plasters, oils
etc., were also left in the care of a few old women in the neighbourhood in
case of urgent need.

On one occasion one of the doctors was called to attend a man whose arm had been cut off. He had been sitting asleep, and probably drunk, on the seat in front of the starting handles of a blast engine. The air pump rod passed through the iron floor plates and a projecting cotter pin also passed through a slot just large enough to take it. The man fell off the bench on the upstroke of the engine with his arm across the slot and the descent of the cotter pin cut it off just above the wrist. He struggled forward and the descending cotter cut off another length.

The doctor had to amputate the limb a third time and the unfortunate patient was ordered to bed on which he said, 'Oh Dr Steel, let me sit up and have my pipe first.'

> *Dr Richard Steel became the first resident medical man in Blaenavon. He was an able and clever doctor. He had four sons, three of whom (Samuel, Richard and William) were among the most excellent medical men ever seen in Blaenavon; the other (Henry) has been the land and house agent here for nearly 40 years.*

Lewis Browning 1906

Memorial to Dr Samuel Elmes Steel in St Peter's Church, Blaenavon

In the churchyard can be seen five rectangular chest tombs of stone with cast iron lids. These include the tomb of Samuel Hopkins (4m from the south side of the church). The lid has decorated edging and the inscription plaque is now inside the church. The other tombs commemorate Sarah Bissell, Thomas Deakin, and Anne Griffiths but the fifth is illegible.

This is the chest tomb of Thomas Deakin who first came to Blaenavon in 1798 at the age of 22. He impressed Samuel Hopkins who made him the Company Mine Agent. He was also a skilled surveyor and of special interest is a map that he made of Blaenavon in 1819 (now held at the County Record Office in Cwmbran). The inscriptions on his tomb reveal that he was married three times, but his third wife outlived him by 13 years.

Side 1 - In Memory of Elizabeth wife of Thomas Deakin. She died July 2nd 1832 aged 56 years. Also, Mary daughter of the above died December 1815 aged 6 years.

Side 2 - In Memory of Elizabeth widow of the said Thomas Deakin who died November 18th 1864 aged 56 years.

Side 3 - Thomas Deakin, born May 3rd 1771, died June 21st 1851.

Side 4 - In Memory of Anne wife of Thomas Deakin who died February 3rd 1834 aged 51 years.

The iron slab on the top of this chest tomb commemorates Sarah Bissell who died on 22nd November 1809, aged 84 years.

St Peter's Churchyard contains a large number of interesting gravestones marking the resting places of Blaenavon folk who played an important part in the social and industrial history of this town.

William Browning mentioned on the left side of this stone was the brother of Lewis Browning and the eldest son of William and Margaret Browning. In 1837 he met with an accident in the Garn Pit Colliery and was severely injured. The inscription reads:

'To the memory of William Browning of this place who died 24th October 1852, aged 33 years. To the memory of Sarah, wife of William Browning of this place who departed this life June 20th 1842 aged 22 years. Also Margaret their daughter died Aug 18th, 1842 aged 3 days.'

William's brother Lewis Browning, the Blaenavon historian, was born at No. 4 Bunker's Hill, Blaenavon on 24th July 1828. The family later moved to Greenland Row.

> *My grandfather (Thomas Browning) hearing of the works starting in Blaenavon, came here with his family in 1787. His son William Browning ... had five boys and three girls, and I am one of these boys. Thomas Browning had to haul stone to build No 1 Furnace when he came from the Forest of Dean, the workmen flocking into the place faster than they were needed.*

> Lewis Browning 1906

97

The Workmen's Hall and Institute

The impressive building opposite St Peter's Church is the Workmen's Hall and Institute which used to play a very important role in the social life of Blaenavon folk. Its construction was envisaged in 1882 when a small number of working men decided to form a committee to investigate the feasibility of providing the town with a permanent institute, where leisure time relaxation and recreation could take place. Premises suitable for this purpose were initially opened in Lion Street in 1883. The institute was financed by a halfpenny per week contribution by the members while the Blaenavon Company provided books for the library and the first billiard table. Within a few years it became apparent that a larger building was needed.

The Blaenavon Company were happy to provide a site free of charge but, due to legal problems, this was not possible so they sold the land to the Trustees for £600 and then returned £500 as a donation. The Blaenavon workers continued to contribute a halfpenny a week from their wages towards the £10,000 cost of the building which was designed by Newport architect E. A. Lansdowne. In August 1893 John Morgan, a local builder began construction with voluntary assistance being given by employees of the Blaenavon Company.

Councillor Robert Kennard JP., son of the Chairman of the Blaenavon Company laid the foundation stone in the presence of an estimated crowd of 7,000 people. Beneath the foundation stone a hermetically sealed box was placed, containing current copies of *The Times*, *Western Mail*, and the *South Wales Daily News*, examples of current coins of the realm minted in 1893, photographs of the Queen, the Prince and Princess of Wales, the Duke and Duchess of York, of Mr Kennard, the Chairman of the Blaenavon Company Ltd., of Mr R.W. Kennard and one of the Institute Committee.

The building bears the date 1894 but it was not until the 7th of January 1895 that Councillor R.W. Kennard returned to perform the opening ceremony following the completion of the building after seventeen months. On the ground floor the rooms consisted of library containing about 4,000 books, newspaper room, magazine room, recreation room and billiard room. There were also committee rooms, a Board Room and toilets. The Hall on the upper floor measured 86 feet by 50 feet and with the wide balcony was capable of seating 1,500 people. It was used largely for concerts, eisteddfods, tea parties, bazaars and political gatherings. Over the years many changes have been made to the interior while the exterior remains largely unaltered. In 1995 the Workmen's Hall celebrated its 100th birthday and after extensive renovations a gala concert was held to celebrate.

Blaenavon Workmen's Hall and Institute opened in 1895 and was one of the finest of its kind in the country. It was financed by weekly contributions from local miners and steel-workers. This building was once the centre of all local cultural, educational and recreational activity in Blaenavon. Entertainment here has passed through the era of the magic lantern to the electrically operated movies when the main hall became a cinema. (The hall is open Monday to Friday, 5.30pm to 9.30pm).

Prince Street Post Office is an impressive Grade II listed building erected in 1937 and still contains its original post office clock

The Co-operative Society building in Ivor Street was built by the Blaenavon Co-operative Society which was formed in 1889 with their original store open in May of that year. A few weeks later deliveries were being made by cart to customers. The Society moved into the purpose-built premises in Ivor Street in 1893. It was rebuilt in 1928 after being damaged by a fire.

Buildings of Interest in the Town Centre

1. Ironworks and Stack Square
2. Ty Mawr
3. Iron Bridge
4. The Lodge
5. St Peter's Schools
6. Vipond House
7. Park St Methodist Church
8. Old Wesleyan School
9. Park House
10. Police Station
11. Workmen's Hall & Institute
12. St Peter's Church
13. Horeb Chapel
14. Post Office
15. Co-operative Building
16. Ebenezer Chapel
17. Bethlehem Chapel
18. Moriah Chapel
19. Old Council Offices
20. Bethel Chapel
21. St Felix Church and School
22. St Paul's Church

Typical happenings in Blaenavon

In January 1860 two Blaenavon workmen, one named Ben Andrews and the other bearing the nickname of 'Strawhat' began the New Year with a bare fisted match of £1 a side. After fighting for two hours and twenty minutes they were unable to decide which was the better man, so each took his own money and was led home by his friends. Ben was blinded and much disfigured about his face while 'Strawhat' was equally punished about the body.

In August 1870 there was a great demonstration in Blaenavon to welcome home Mr E. Kennard and his bride. Banners and flags, processions, addresses, horse and foot races, rustic sports, acrobatic performances and fireworks made a grand gala-day of it. The Cyfarthfa and Blaenavon band attended and about 12,000 people were present.

In 1880 a Blaenavon man who visited the Bath & West of England Show had rather too much to drink. He had to be helped into a train and arrived at Blaenavon in the brake van labelled on his back, 'This side up - drunk.'

Blaenavon barbers in 1890 raised the price of men's haircuts to 3d and shaving to 1d. But the customers of one barber refused to pay the new 'extortionate' rates, forcing the unhappy man to revert to the old prices. Within a few hours, the rest of the profession in the town, followed his 'black-legging' example.

In January 1935, William Royal, an employee of Blaenavon Co-operative Society was driving a horse and bread van up the road leading to Old Houses, Garn-yr-erw, when the road caved in and the horse was swallowed up in the deep hole. The slip was probably caused by heavy rains having partly undermined the road. William escaped by jumping to one side, but it was some hours before the horse could be rescued.

Six Blaenavon people were injured and a number of others cut and bruised in August 1946, when the entire floor of a room at the Queen Victoria Inn, Garnddyrys, collapsed at about 10.15 pm on a Saturday night. About thirty people in the room were precipitated nine feet into the cellar of the inn.

According to a gravestone in St Peter's churchyard a '124 year old' man, who had died 94 years previously, still had six years to live (in 1968). Walter Pearson Follet died in 1874 at the age of 30, but instead of that date appearing on the gravestone, a mistake was made and 1974 inscribed.

The Streets of Blaenavon

I remember, too, the cold of the early morning tubs, with the wind coming down from the Coity tearing at my trews; the frosty walks home from Garndyrus with my father; the dreary quiet of Hush Silence Street and the little square windows loaded with ice; the lights coming from the Drum and Monkey where the men were putting away the beer and quarrelling about unions.

Alexander Cordell
Rape of the Fair Country 1959

Many of the old streets of the town once had different names to those by which they are now known. King Street was formerly Heol-ust-tewi (Hush-silence-road); Broad Street bore the name Heol-y-nant (Brook Street), because a brook ran down from the Bridgend underneath the buildings down to the Afon Lwyd. It was a narrow lane with a house here and there and bounded by a low wall about two feet high or a shabby thorn hedge between it and the brook. Hill Street was once very stony, crooked and narrow, known by the Welsh speaking locals as Heol Garegog. Originally it was just a path across a field used by the night workers, and therefore known as Llwybr Rhyd-y-nos - 'Along by night path'.

Park Street was originally called Beaufort Street and Burford Street is probably a corruption of the same name. The central streets of the town are patriotically called King, Queen and Prince Street, with a High Street slotted in among the royal names. A good sense of humour has always prevailed in the town. This gave rise to the junction of Old and New William Street with Lower Hill Street, being christened 'Coffin Corner,'- it was here that Mr Thomas the undertaker had his premises. Likewise the Hallelujah lamppost at the junction of Prince Street, Broad Street and Albert Street served as a religious meeting place and the Salvation Army band often played beneath the light. The junction of Broad Street, Commercial Street and Old William Street was known as 'The Cross'.

The main thoroughfare in the town, which is lined with shops, is Broad Street and this was laid out in 1875 as the result of the enterprise of J.G. Williams, a local businessman, who also provided Blaenavon with its first residential hotel, a gas works, paved roads, assembly rooms and a brewery. He also erected an indoor market (no longer existing), after which Market Street was named.

Broad Street and the adjacent terraces, with views to the nearby mountain, provide a fine example of the traditional townscape of a South Wales valley-head settlement.

Blaenavon's first market had been in the open air opposite Engine Row, and here vegetables and fruit could be bought in abundance. Farmers and other traders also brought in butter, cheese, sheep, pigs, meat of all kinds, shoes and flannel.

Lion Square near the old Council offices used to be the venue for many of the town's open-air, public and official functions. The old Volunteers would assemble there for ceremonial parades and then return for dismissal, brightening the rather dismal surroundings with their scarlet tunics. All sorts of travelling shows also made their stand on the Square. These consisted of roundabouts, swings, side shows with fat-ladies, fire-eaters, flea circuses, cocoa-nut shies and all the fun of the fair.

Steam organs would grind out mechanical music to be replaced in later years by music blared out from loud speakers. There were wild beast shows, boxing booths, travelling theatres and quack doctors who could extract teeth or cure any complaint under the sun.

In later years the Square was then used, mostly on Fridays, as an open-air market. It was purchased by the Urban Council in 1961 and the open market was no longer allowed. The Square then was used as a more or less unauthorised bus and car park.

A view from the Ironworks down North Street showing a large number of the old houses which were demolished during a period of slum clearance in the 1970s

105

A pub for every week of the year !

At one time it used to be a proud boast that Blaenavon had so many public houses that it was possible to drink in a different one every week of the year. The first tavern in the town was the old Crown Inn which stood in North Street, below Ty Mawr. A sign over the door declared that it was the 'Old Crown' but it later became better known as 'The Drum and Monkey.' It must have been a very lively place for the furnace workers in particular drank a considerable quantity of beer and it is said that before the end of most nights there were often two or three men installed in the nearby stocks, for creating a disturbance.

Blaenavon's lost pubs include: The Albert Inn, Alma, Belle Vue, Boot, Brittania, Brewery Vaults, Bridgend, Crown Inn, Drum and Monkey, Forge Hammer, Forresters, Globe, Greyhound, Griffin, Ivor Castle, Jolly Colliers, King's Arms, King's Head, Lamb Inn, Miner's Arms, Mount Pleasant, Nag's Head, New Inn, New King's Arms, Old Duke, Old Lion Vaults, Old Railway, Oxford, Pen Cefyl, Prince of Wales, Railway, Rising Sun, Rock and Fountain, Royal Arms, Royal Exchange, Royal George, Royal Oak, Star, Swan, Three Cranes, Vine Tree, White Hart, White Horse, White Lion and Winning Horse.

The Rolling Mill in Broad Street is one of Blaenavon's surviving public houses

106

Keeping the Peace

The most serious disturbance in the town occurred in 1868 when riots broke out following a General Election. The unpopular Tory MPs for Monmouthshire had been challenged by Colonel Harry Clifford, who was a Liberal and regarded as a hero by the working class for daring to stand against the other candidates. The *Pontypool Free Press* reported that:-

> *Riots broke out at various places in Monmouthshire after the declaration of the poll in the Parliamentary General Election, in which Octavius Morgan polled 3,761 votes, Poulett Somerset 3,525 and Henry Morgan Clifford (Liberal) 2,338. The first two, both Conservatives, were declared elected. The valley towns voted over-whelmingly for the Liberal candidate.*

Violence in Blaenavon started in a pub in King Street and then various shops and hotels in the town owned by Tory locals were attacked. The mob then moved on to J.G. Williams's Lion Hotel which was regarded as the Tory Party HQ in Blaenavon. A full scale siege developed with doors battered down and every window smashed. The street outside was crowded with people looking on while the rioters flung all kinds of items through windows and doorways. Costly furniture and other articles were taken into a house nearby which was being constructed and these items were set on fire. Shelves, dressers, chests of drawers, beds and bedsteads, piano, organ, tables and chairs were all destroyed. Barrels of beer were rolled outside and sent flying down the main street and containers of spirits and cider were taken away.

Moving on to the Prince of Wales, the mob smashed doors and windows, drank or destroyed all the liquor or beer, carried away all the money they could find, as well as several flitches of bacon. The looting and rioting only ended when a detachment of the 23rd Royal Welsh Fusiliers arrived to reinforce the police and numerous arrests were made. When order was at last restored the local magistrate, Mr T.W. Kennard, who lived at Ty Mawr, read the Riot Act.

The men arrested were later tried at Monmouth Assizes by Mr Justice Keating. In his summing up he said that the riots were disgraceful and that 'It was a monstrous proposition when people were not allowed to entertain and express their political opinions in a free country.' Sentences varying from four to twelve months hard labour were given to 36 men who were charged with riot and demolishing property at Abersychan and Blaenavon.

A re-enactment of the 1868 riot was held in 2001

The Lion Hotel in Broad Street was extensively damaged by the rioters

Detachment of the 23rd Royal Welsh Fusiliers arriving to reinforce the police

The Police Station in Church Street was built by the Ironworks Company in 1867. The adjoining courthouse which used to stand on the uphill side was used by the Urban District Council as a meeting place before the Workmen's Hall was built.

A Chapel on every Corner

The establishment of chapels in Blaenavon began as a result of the Methodist Revival in the 18th century when meetings were held from about 1780 in an ancient farmhouse known as 'Y Persondy' (The Parsonage). Howell Harris, the famous Welsh Calvinistic Methodist, and Edmund Jones of the Tranch (near Pontypool) are said to have preached there. About this time the Calvinistic Methodists erected the first place of worship in the rapidly growing small town. It was called Capel-y-graig and it existed until 1814 when owing to its close proximity to the blast furnaces, and being in the way of the development of the Ironworks, a new site was granted by Messrs Hill and Hopkins, on which Penuel Calvinistic Methodist Church was built in 1815.

Situated at the top of King Street this was Blaenavon's oldest Noncomformist Church and it held its last service in January 1968. Its closure was caused by the subsidence of the late 19th century schoolroom. The whole building was declared unsafe and the Monmouthshire Presbytery decided to demolish the entire property in view of the high cost of repairs. A notable member of this church at one time was Miss Hattie Harris who became Mrs Arthur Jenkins, wife of the Pontypool MP and mother of Roy Jenkins, who also entered Parliament and is now Lord Jenkins.

In 1790 the Baptist cause had its beginnings in the town with meetings held in the homes of William and Francis James, leading to the erection of the first Baptist Chapel in James Street in 1805. The building had an interesting history, for after the Baptists had finished with it, the Wesleyans made use of the building; then the Welsh Congregationalists, and finally the Salvation Army.

Following a disagreement with their brethren about a change of minister, a branch from Horeb Chapel was formed in 1825 by 81 members. They built Ebenezer Chapel the following year on land leased from Francis James, who gave his name to Old James Street.

Bethlehem Chapel, built by the Congregationalists, was so-named because it was opened on Christmas Day 1820. It stood just below the later Great Western Railway Station and was eventually abandoned in 1842, as being inconveniently situated, and the congregation moved to a new chapel in Broad Street, also called Bethlehem. Moriah Chapel which stands in the centre of Broad Street was originally known as Broad Street Baptist Chapel and built in 1844.

In 1823 Hugh Bourne walked across the Black Mountains from Herefordshire to preach in Blaenavon and shortly afterwards a Primitive Methodist Society was formed in the town.

By 1830 a Methodist chapel was opened in King Street and when the congregation became too big it was sold in 1878 to the Baptists for £500. The following year the Primitive Methodist Society opened their new church. Designed by James Hicks of Bristol it was built in the Gothic style by John Burgoyne, a Beaufort builder, at a cost of £3,600. It finally closed in September 1966 when its members were unable to meet the rising costs of the maintenance of such a large building.

The first Wesleyan Chapel in Blaenavon was built in 1837. On each side of the building were rows of houses which appropriately became known as Chapel Row. The site of these long demolished buildings is now part of the Gilchrist Thomas Industrial Estate.

The Congregational Church was founded in 1863 and its members first met in Market Street and then James Street Chapel. Lion Street Congregational Chapel was built in 1867 at a cost of £900 and it catered for the non-Welsh speaking people who had come to Blaenavon in search of employment.

By 1900 there were thirteen chapels in Blaenavon and the services were all being held in English. The census of 1901 recorded a population of 10,010, of whom 857 or 8% were Welsh speakers. Ten years later the population had reached 11,087, of whom only 616 or 5% were Welsh speakers.

Bethlehem Chapel in Broad Street was built in the Classical style in 1842, but the congregation of Welsh-speaking independents first met in an earlier building on Christmas Day in 1820. Inside is a gallery supported on light cast iron pillars.

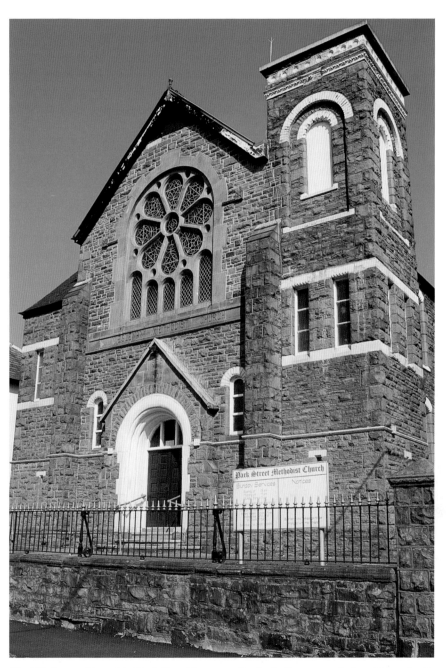

The Wesleyan Chapel in Park Street has a particularly fine rose window. It was built in 1885 by John Wills of Derby.

Moriah Chapel in Broad Street dates from 1888 and is in the Classical style, but has an ornate interior. Iron columns with gold painted spiral decoration support a gallery with pierced ironwork balustrades, reached by twin staircases from the entrance vestibule.

In Church Street close to the Workmen's Hall, is Horeb Chapel which was built in 1862, by Thomas Thomas, a Blaenavon civil engineer, to accommodate a congregation whose origins went back to 1807. The entrance is distinctive with its stone portico supported by Ionic columns while the round headed side windows are typical of the period. Inside are galleries supported on cast iron pillars on three sides of the building. A baptismal pool remains below the floorboards.

St Paul's Church at the corner of Llanover Road and Bryn Terrace was built of stone in 1893 from the ruins of Capel Newydd on a site which was donated by the Blaenavon Company and the Marquis of Abergavenny. The foundation stone was laid in 1893 by Mr. R.W. Kennard JP. In November 1953 the church celebrated 60 years service. Relics from Capel Newydd to be seen in this church include the old iron key to the door, a stone altar, reredos, the entrance keystone and a Welsh Bible.

The stone altar from Capel Newydd can be seen in St Paul's Church

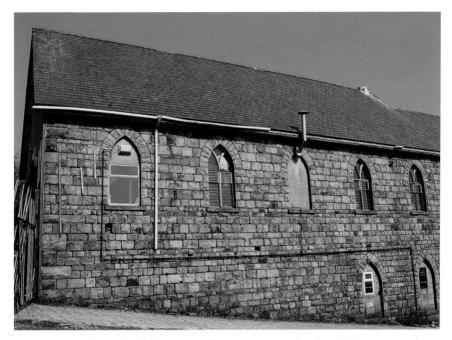

St James Church was built beside the Abergavenny road at Cae White, as a replacement for the old St James 'Iron' Church. The stone used was taken from the disused ironworks furnaces in North Street. Voluntary labour was provided by the male members of the congregation who carried out all the excavations for the foundations and also hauled the stone to the site, which was provided by the Blaenavon Company. The contract for building the new church was awarded to Isaac Edmunds, a Blaenavon man, whose tender was £1,600. He completed the work within twelve months and the new St James church was dedicated in 1914, with the Rev Watkin Edwards appointed as the first minister.

The old bell that used to hang at the iron church was installed in the new building and when that in turn became disused in 1970, it was transferred to St Paul's Church in Llanover Road.

VANISHED BLAENAVON

What is there, I wonder in the sagging bricks and mortar of a little town that clutches at the heart? Like the Waun Mary Gunter, the Hill Pit cottages near Garn-yr-erw; Stable Row where the farrier and ostlers lived, Engine Row where lived the engineers....

Alexander Cordell
This Proud and Savage Land (1986)

From about 1817 to the mid 1830s the Blaenavon Company had embarked on a fairly determined programme of house building in order to accommodate their ever-growing workforce. They constructed terraced houses, consisting of about thirty dwellings in batches of five. Downstairs was a living room, a small pantry and a back room and on the first floor an unpartitioned bedroom. The walls were lime-plastered and colour-washed.

Each row of cottages was occupied by a particular group of workers according to their trade: River Row, Quick Building and Bunker's Row were where the colliers and miners lived; cokers and coke-setters lived in Coaltar Row and Upper Stable Houses were occupied by stable-men, hauliers and coachmen and Stable Yard by ostlers. In the second half of the 19th century, the drivers of steam locomotives joined the aristocrats of the labour force and resided in Engine Row.

Unfortunately a large number of the old buildings associated with Blaenavon's ironworks and collieries have been demolished over the years and these include such historic structures as the laboratory used by the Gilchrist cousins and the mid-19th century offices of the old Blaenavon Iron & Coal Company. By 1901 there were almost six hundred cottages and houses owned by the Blaenavon Company and in the years following the Second World War these dwellings, although in a poor state, were still occupied. The low rents charged by the Company no doubt made the tenants very reluctant to move into modern houses for which they would have to pay a higher rent. But when the Coal Board took over these properties, many of which lay outside the town, the tenants were forced to leave and the cottages were gradually demolished.

During this period of demolition and slum clearance many of the old terraced houses were replaced with new Council estates, on the edge of the town and included Elgam, Capel Newydd, Heol-y-parc, Hillside, Ty Fry, Avon Road, Riverside, Kennard Court and Kennard Crescent.

As there were no building restrictions, houses could be put up in any fashion so they were often built back to back. There were no regulations to prevent overcrowding as shown by a report of 1830 which listed one house with seventeen people residing in a single room. No consideration was given to providing main drainage or sanitation and as there were no arrangements for disposing of household refuse it accumulated in the streets in great heaps. It is not surprising that outbreaks of disease frequently occurred.

> *A typical worker's cottage seldom has more than one room which serves the purpose of living and sleeping. A large dresser and shelves usually form the partition between the two, and where there are separate beds for the family, a curtain or low board is the only division, with no regular partition.*

> Extract from a Report compiled in 1847

Shepherds Square stood at the south end of Staffordshire Row and was built some time before 1812 as an irregular quadrangle of eighteen houses. It was open on the east side to the trailroad leading from the furnaces down to the Monmouthshire canal basin at Pontnewynydd. The cottages were built on three sides of a court and the central space was occupied by communal privies. Demolition took place in June 1970 and the site is now occupied by Kennard Place (SO 249091).

Staffordshire Row was an interesting housing design being a good example of the 'double-house' plan. Two streets were built one above the other into the side of a sloping bank. The lower houses were entered from North Street, the upper dwellings, Staffordshire Row from a higher level at the rear. Each house had just two rooms.

The old 'Lock Up' in North Street was built in 1836 and demolished in 1964. It stood just above the infamous 'Drum and Monkey' Inn which is featured in Alexander Cordell's novel *Rape of the Fair Country.*

The first police officer to come here was Mr Order, in the year 1838; he came to keep order, although we were orderly enough before he came! Some of those who followed him were Merryweather, Owens, Vincent, Coles, Sergeant James, Coombs, Jones and Sergeant Beach.

Lewis Browning 1906

The 'Barracks' was a four storey building which stood behind the Clarence Hotel in King Street. It was built by the Blaenavon Company in 1850 to accommodate 'Redcoat' soldiers. During the bitter coal strike of 1893 a company of the 2nd Devon Regiment was stationed in this building. Later this Company moved to Ebbw Vale where there had been violent clashes between strikers and non-strikers. The 'Barracks' was demolished in 1960.

In the 1840s there were three principle clusters of buildings in the area now occupied by the town, one around the Ironworks, one along the east-west axis, now King Street, where any pre-industrial settlement was probably concentrated, and one around St Peter's Church. The spaces between the three nuclei were gradually filled with buildings which evolved into a recognisable town by the 1850s. A significant development was the naming of the streets in the 1860s.

Nomination Document 2000

The rear of Staffordshire Row with the former general offices of the Blaenavon Company perched on the high ground above

The old Company Stables and animal surgery as seen in the late 1950s before subsequent demolition

Bunker's Row (SO 252094) was built in about 1792 at the same time as Stack Square. It was originally known as Bunker's Hill and consisted of twenty houses built back to back in two rows of ten to provide accommodation for the lower paid workers. These buildings overlooked the Company Stables and stood opposite the existing Rifleman's Arms. Each house had just one room downstairs, measuring 10 ft by 11 ft and there was a loft bedroom accessed by a ladder-type stairs. In about 1860 improvements were carried out to the houses and some years later the back-to-back pairs were converted into single houses. They were demolished in October 1972 having survived for 180 years.

Chapel Row (SO 244109) used to stand on the site of the present day Gilchrist Thomas Industrial Estate, through which one passes on the way to Big Pit National Mining Museum. It was an isolated terrace built by the Blaenavon Iron and Coal Company in 1839. There were forty houses in two adjoining rows and in the middle was a large Wesleyan chapel which was one of the oldest Methodist chapels in the valley. Furnace slag tipped on land behind the row gradually began to dangerously encroach upon the cottages and ten of them were abandoned in 1910. The others survived until demolition in 1971.

> *The Blaenavon Company needed more dwellings, so they built the new Wesleyan Chapel between two rows of houses, which came to be called Chapel Row. It was largely through the influence of Mr Thomas Deakin, the coal and mine manager, who was a Wesleyan, that the new chapel was built.*

Lewis Browning 1906

The old St James Church stood near Victoria Row, off the Garn Road, in the centre of a field and beside a small canal which ran from Garn-yr-erw to Blaenavon Ironworks. It was generally referred to as the 'Iron Church' but was actually a wooden structure, lined inside with matchwood while the outer skin was made of zinc sheets. Waste tipped from the North Street furnaces encroached on the building and it was eventually closed. A local butcher who had a use for the timber bought the abandoned building for just £20. The site was eventually covered by a slag tip which was removed during a land reclamation scheme in the 1970s and the Gilchrist Thomas Industrial Estate established.

This drawing by William Byrne, based on a sketch by Sir Richard Colt Hoare (August 1798), shows a covered bridge supported by ten arches, which had been converted into dwellings for industrial workers.

> *The want of habitations for the increasing number of families, had occasioned an ingenious contrivance: a bridge being drawn across a deep dingle for the support of a railroad leading into a mine, the arches, which are ten in number, have been walled up, and formed into dwellings.*

William Coxe 1801

In April 2000 the U.K. Television Channel Four 'Time Team' spent three days searching for the remains of this 18th century structure, believed to be the world's first iron railed railway viaduct. While the foundations of nearby Coaltar Row were being carefully revealed by pick and shovel, two large JCBs dug massive holes some 15 metres deep in the search for the lost viaduct.

The project was considerably hampered by the weather, for it proved to be the wettest April on record, but just as filming was due to come to an end, they broke through a stone roof. A camera fastened to the end of a long pole revealed what appeared to be the interior of the covered roof on top of the viaduct. The massive hole was later filled in and the lost viaduct remains to be revealed one day in the future.

Brick House used to stand on Bunker's Hill near the old brick-works

A wall near the site of Brick Cottage is built out of Bessemer tuyeres

Significant dates in the history of Blaenavon Town

1782	Blaenavon Coal & Iron Company founded
1783	North Street, King Street and Bunker's Hill developed
1789	Blaenavon Ironworks commenced operating
1795	Monmouthshire Canal completed
	Tramroad from Blaenavon to Pontnewynydd constructed
1798	Capel-y-graig founded
	William Coxe visited Blaenavon
1802	Monmouthshire Canal extended to Pontnewynydd
1805	St Peter's Church opened
1815	Penuel Calvinistic Methodist Chapel built in King Street
1816	St Peter's School opened by Sarah Hopkins
1823	Horeb Baptist Chapel opened in Old James Street
1825	Turnpike road from Blaenavon to Abergavenny constructed
1826	Ebenezer Chapel built
1837	Wesleyan Chapel built
1838	'Lock Up' built at the north end of Staffordshire Row
1839	Chapel Row built either side of the Weslyan Chapel
1842	Bethlehem Chapel built in Broad Street
1850	'The Barracks' erected behind Upper King Street
	Dyne Steel Incline constructed
1854	Blaenavon to Pontypool railway opened
1860	Blaenavon adopted the Local Government Act of 1858 and the streets of Blaenavon were given names
1861	Capel Newydd was abandoned
1862	Town Hall opened in Lion Street
1863	Foundation of the Congregational Church
	Horeb Baptist Chapel opened for divine service
1864	Blaenavon Company constructed 100 workmen's cottages
1867	Gas pipes laid in the town by the Blaenavon Gas Company
1868	Riots in the town following General Election
1870	LNWR Station opened
1874	Blaenavon lit by gas for the first time
1875	Broad Street established by J.G. Williams
1878	Blaenavon-Talywain railway completed
1880	Blaenavon Ironworks rated the most modern in the world
1883	Hospital established for employees of the Blaenavon Company
1884	Corps of the Salvation Army established
1885	Construction of Wesleyan Chapel in Park Street
1889	Blaenavon Co-operative Society founded
1893	Construction of St Paul's Church
1894	Construction of Police Station and Court in Church Road
1895	Blaenavon Workmen's Hall & Institute opened
1904	Hillside School built in Upper Hill Street
1905	Establishment of a branch of St John's Ambulance Brigade

1909	Blaenavon Conservative Club formally opened
1913	New St James Church opened on the Abergavenny Road
1914	Blaenavon Council bought Elgam Farm as site for 50 houses
1919	Elgam Housing Estate constructed
1921	New Recreation Ground opened
1923	Open air swimming pool constructed
1925	Ty Mawr taken over by the Blaenavon Medical Society
1930	New Council offices built in Lion Street
1933	Electricity becomes available in Blaenavon
1936	King Edward VIII visited Blaenavon
1937	New Post Office opened
	Park Street Senior School opened
1938	New Fire Station officially opened
1939	A division of the Red Cross Society formed
1940	Debt on the Workmen's Hall cleared
1945	Golden Jubilee of Workmen's Hall celebrated
1959	Publication of *Rape of the Fair Country* by Alexander Cordell
1961	New Fire Station opened at Cae White
1963	Queen Elizabeth and Prince Philip visited Blaenavon
1969	Pipes laid through the town for North Sea Gas
	Blaenavon's first ever Carnival held
1970	Re-development of Albert Street and Corn Street
	Arthur Jenkins Home for the aged opened by Roy Jenkins MP
1971	New Health Centre opened
	Gilchrist Thomas Industrial Estate commenced
1974	New heated indoor swimming pool opened
	Blaenavon's first-ever mayor was elected
1976	New Leisure Centre opened at a cost of £188,000
1980	Big Pit closed
1981	Prince Charles visited Blaenavon Ironworks and Big Pit
1983	Big Pit Mining Museum opened
1984	Workmen's Hall declared unsafe and closed
1985	Blaenavon twinned with Coutras in Aquitaine, France
1986	First 'America Week' held in the town
1989	Bi-centenary of Blaenavon Ironworks celebrated
1990	Workmen's Hall re-opened after expensive repair work
1992	Blaenavon's Community Woodland site opened
1994	Centenary celebrations of Workmen's Hall
1998	Official opening of Garn Lakes
1999	Blaenavon nominated as a World Heritage Site
2000	Blaenavon declared a World Heritage Site
2001	Big Pit became the Welsh National Mining Museum

WALK TWO

Forgeside, Big Pit and Garn-yr-erw

7.2km (4. 5 miles)

START: Blaenavon Ironworks Car Park (SO 248092)

Descend the steps at the end of the car park and turn right to follow the pavement. Just past Kennard Place turn right down the road leading past the Blaenavon Health Care Unit. Go down a narrow fenced path on the left and then left along the road for a short distance to turn right over an old iron bridge, spanning the Afon Lwyd.

Head up to a road and turn left. Shortly cross the road to ascend some steps to follow a fenced path. Across to the left can now be seen Glantorfaen House which was Blaenavon's first vicarage.

Glantorfaen House was built at the beginning of the 19th century on Allgood Farm land which once covered an area of 125 acres, the farm was established in 1670. The Blaenavon Company purchased the house from Edward Lewis in 1819 but he continued to live there until his death in 1838. It then became the town's first vicarage, being occupied by the the Rev John Jones until his death in 1885. The house was later used by a succession of managers of the Blaenavon Company.

129

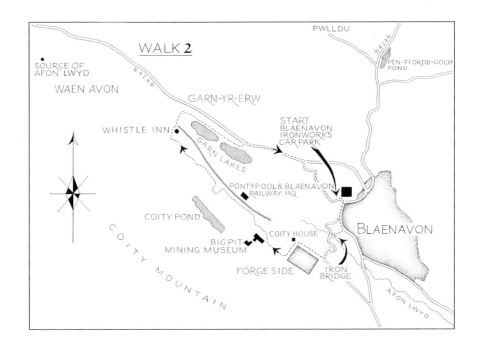

In the late 1850s the Blaenavon Company established a new iron-works on the opposite side of the valley from its original furnaces at a site which became known as Forgeside and rolling mills were moved here from Garnddyrys. The new works was able to make up to 500 tons a week of iron rails, tyres for railway waggons and carriages, and plates for boilers and ships. In 1868 the first of several blast furnaces on the site was blown in, and five years after this there were at the two sites ten blast furnaces, 89 puddling furnaces and eight rolling mills.

The Forgeside works continues to operate on a modest scale in new buildings and parts of the original tyre mills. Others of the early buildings remaining are Coity House, probably built between about 1840 and 1860 for the works manager, a power station of about 1920, and most of the workers' housing.

World Heritage Industrial Landscape
Nomination Document 2000

This iron bridge (SO 248088) comprises three cast iron arch beams supporting wrought iron deck plates. A modern bridge has been erected on the original one to carry a footpath over the Afon Lwyd.

The stone-lined entrance to Aaron Brute's Level lies low down in a hedge about 60m from the cast-iron tramroad bridge which connected the level to the ironworks. The owner Aaron Brute was of the Llanbedr family of stonemasons and an example of his work (signed A. Brute) can be seen at Partrishow Church in the Black Mountains. On moving to Blaenavon he became a mine owner, a building contractor and is also known to have been a Calvinistic preacher. His level which produced iron ore ceased working by 1843.

> *Mr Aaron Brute... is well-known and will continue to be so for some time to come, for there are houses, a level and a well named after him; his tomb-stone too will keep him in memory. He died the year following the building of St Peter's Church.*

Lewis Browning 1906

On joining a road, turn right to go across a bridge over the High Level LNWR Railway. At the T junction turn right along the road leading to Forgeside.

The first stone building on the left used to be a public house called 'The Footballer's Arms' as a tribute to Ken Jones a well-known rugby hero and Olympic athlete who was born in Blaenavon. In 1960 he was awarded the OBE in recognition of his many sporting achievements. He had won 16 Welsh Championship Gold Medals and 44 International Caps, playing for Wales. In 1948 he represented Great Britain in the Olympic Games at Wembley in London and ran in the second leg in the 4 x 100 metres in which BRitain was placed second to the USA. In addition he had captained the British team in the 1954 Berne European Games and in the same year represented Wales in the Empire and Commonwealth Games at Vancouver, where he gained a bronze medal in the 220 yards.

The old Forgeside School is shortly passed on the left and next to it is Zion Baptist Chapel. Gething Terrace is named after a young furnaceman who became manager of the old furnaces and later managed the blast furnaces at Forgeside. He was also a founder member of the Workmen's Institute and the Blaenavon Cooperative Society.

Zion Baptist Church was built in 1875 at a cost of £650 to serve the growing population of Forgeside. Its mother church was the English Baptist Chapel in Broad Street, Blaenavon.

Walk on to the end of the road where a set of iron gates provide a view into the Doncaster Works which stand on the site of the old Forgeside Ironworks which opened in1860. It had many advantages over the old North Street Ironworks. There was much more space for future expansion on a level site and was linked by steam railway to Pontypool and Newport. The Garnddyrys Forge had proved very inconvenient being so far from the old Ironworks and also the distance from Garnddyrys to Newport via the difficult and dangerous inclines and the slow canal was 26 miles. By comparison it was just 16 miles from Forgeside to Newport by the new railway down the eastern Valley.

A vast sum of money was spent on establishing this new Works, with the plant consisting of six hot-blast furnaces, puddling furnaces, rolling mills and also a tyre mill which was built to produce wheels for railway rolling stock. This new works was built on freehold land which meant that there was no requirement for the Company to pay ground rent.

The erection of Bessemer convertors at Forgeside was very costly. However, the Blaenavon Company was able to find the money, and between 1874 and 1880 brought the works into line with most of their competitors.

Forgeside village was built to house the ironworkers and those employed at the nearby collieries. The dwellings were in due course complemented by shops, a school and a public house, thus making the village self-contained.

By 1880 the plant had been developed to such a standard that it was regarded as the most modern ironworks in the world. In that year Blaenavon was described as 'a place with an extensive ironworks, abundant collieries, seven blast furnaces and three rolling mills for heavy and light rails, and four brick factories.' However, after World War I the decline in the demand for coal and steel favoured centres closer to the markets.

The last furnace at Forgeside was extinguished in 1938. As usual it was all a question of economics. The local reserves of iron ore had long been depleted and the cost of transporting imported ore from the coast had become too expensive. The future now lay in the erection of new large steel works in the coastal regions of South Wales.

R.W. Kennard was elected Chairman of the Blaenavon Company in 1903. It was his son T.W. Kennard who built Crumlin Viaduct. Another son was H. M. Kennard who also became a chief shareholder in the Blaenavon Company Ltd. His death in London in August 1911 at the age of 78, heralded the end of the Kennard era which had started in 1836. For nearly three-quarters of a century, through four generations the Kennard family had controlled and guided the fortunes of Blaenavon. Today, their name is kept alive by the groups of houses built in 1973 along Church Road and named Kennard Court, Kennard Crescent and Kennard Place. The town also adopted the Kennard family motto: *Sped spes non fracta* - 'But hope is not broken' - which appears on the family crest.

In 1938, the Company finally closed down the plant. Deep gloom settled over the steel town of Blaenavon and the ghostly spectre of unemployment roamed the streets of the hill town which formerly had echoed and rang with the noise and bustle of hundreds of workers.

Tom Grey Davies 1973

Turn left at the end of Gething Terrace and then go immediately right.
At the end of this road, behind a pair of iron gates, can be seen Coity House
(SO 242089). This was built in 1860 to accommodate the Manager of the
Blaenavon Iron & Steel Company. At the end of the 19th century it was
occupied by Captain Percy G. Pennymore, Director of the Blaenavon Gas
and Iron Company. The building later became the general office of Daniel
Doncaster & Sons Ltd., and it was last used in 1990. It is a grade II listed
building and is also known as 'The White House'.

It was Blaenavon's long association with iron and steel-making that
attracted Doncasters to this location in 1957 they took over the old tyre mill
and press shop which had been vacated by the Blaenavon Company. By
1962 they were employing 150 men and looking forward to further
development.

In May 1968 Doncasters opened a new 125 ton rolling mill on the site. It
was the largest rolling mill in Britain specialising in the production of alloy
rings used in the latest jet engines. Rings produced here were used in the
Concorde prototype and in all subsequent Concorde aircraft.

Now turn left and go up beside 'C Row' which is one of five terraces
built at Forgeside by the Blaenavon Company more than a century ago to
house people employed both in the steelworks and the nearby collieries.
Instead of being given names, the terraces were called somewhat
unimaginitively, A Row, B Row, C Row, D Row and E Row. The first two
rows were demolished in 1977, but the other three survive and retain their
original names.

The large red brick building passed on the right was erected in 1920 as
an electricity power house for the Forgeside complex.

Coity House was built in 1860 to provide accommodation for the manager of the Blaenavon Iron & Steel Company. It is now a Listed Building.

Keep straight on and the tarmac road turns into concrete and bends around to the right in the direction of Big Pit (Pwll Mawr). On arriving at the Big Pit Coach Park, follow the road to the right to pass the entrance to this National Mining Museum. (You may like to add an interesting underground extension to the walk. Free admission at the time of writing).

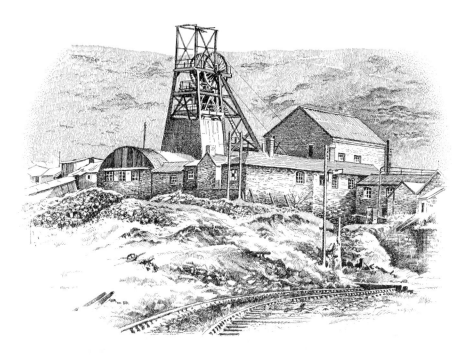

Big Pit was sunk in 1860 and is therefore one of the oldest deep mines in the South Wales Coalfield and incorporates galleries which were worked some years earlier. Its elliptical shape (6 metres across) allowed two trams to be wound side by side - hence 'Big Pit'. It is stone lined for the first ten metres downwards and was used as the downcast shaft with bad air being drawn up the upcast shaft at the earlier Coity Pits.

The shaft of Big Pit (366ft) was sunk precisely on a fault line so that roadways could be driven either side into the Elled (the first seam from the surface), the Three-quarter 15m below (51 ft), followed by Black Vein at 36m below that (120 ft), Meadow Vein at 66m below (219 ft), Old Coal at 89m below (294 ft) and finally Garw 11m below (366 ft).

Two pumps kept the deeper workings clear of water; a Cameron pump with two inverted cylinders and two 6 inch single acting rams forced the water from the workings to the bottom of the pit, where another pump, raised it 50 metres up the shaft to an adit through which it ran off by gravity. This can be found near the site of Engine Pit in the landscaped area below Gilchrist Thomas Industrial Estate.

There were four haulage engines supplied with steam from four Cornish boilers. The winding engines were formerly a pair of 26 inch horizontal cylinders, raising two loaded trams per journey. In 1935 the steam winding engine was replaced by an electrical one installed by the Uskside Engineering Company of Newport and is still in use.

By 1958 Big Pit was employing more than 1,000 men and in 1966 it was the only deep Coal Board mine left in the Blaenavon area. But the Three-quarter seam had been abandoned in 1921, Elled in 1949, Black Vein in 1955, Meadow Vein in 1964 and Old Coal in 1967. This left just the Garw, the lowest coal seam which had a maximum thickness of just 71cm (2ft 4in). It was first class coking coal but so hard that it resisted all attempts at mechanisation. But eventually a plough was installed which successfully cut and loaded the coal on to a chain conveyor.

The face of the Garw seam was 2 miles from the pit head in the direction of Brynmawr. An alternative drift was driven downwards in the vicinity of the washery and from then on the coal was brought out that way. The original shaft was retained for maintenance purposes only. By 1979 just 250 men were employed at the pit, producing about 72,000 tons of coal a year.

Although some mechanisation had been adopted at Big Pit, as the Garw seam became narrower (down to 1 ft t in) the NCB were reluctant to invest further and by 1979 only 250 men were employed producing about 72,000 tons of coal a year and on 2nd February 1980 the pit finally closed.

This large tip used to stand near Big Pit and it was one of three, collectively known as 'Little Egypt'. They were removed in 1979.

The cast iron half wheel which is seen on the approach to Big Pit Mining Museum originally operated a shaft at Celynen North Colliery, Newbridge and on its closure the wheel was presented to Big Pit.

Following closure plans were prepared to preserve the mine as a living monument to the South Wales Coal Industry. It was well suited for this purpose for apart from the interesting underground and surface features, the shaft was not deep, its upper levels drained naturally, gas was not present and ventilation was comparatively simple to maintain.

The steering committee for the £900,000 project considered that as well as giving visitors an authentic impression of the development of coal mining, such a museum would also provide tourist employment for local people and possibly bring some extra revenue for businesses in the town.

On 1st April, 1983, the first tourists entered the cage to descend the 90m shaft and experience an underground tour, led by retired miners who were now employed as guides. During the first year 90,573 visitors were received and within the next few years this figure rose to more than 100,000.

The surface tour includes where the electricians, carpenters and black-smiths once worked. At one time the blacksmiths' shop had nine forges in operation producing all the equipment required and necessary repairs.

The pre-war pithead baths are the only surviving examples with their original internal fittings. Within the complex they include the old canteen, where refreshments are available, and an exhibition area which includes a re-created miner's cottage.

A surface gallery, resembling a drift mine has been constructed to complement the exhibits on the underground tour by showing how the more recent coal cutting techniques employed on more modern faces operate.

The underground tour is the main attraction which enables visitors to experience a ride in the cage to pit bottom and walk through the upper levels where seams of exposed coal can still be seen. Air doors are passed on the way, which more than 100 years ago were operated by young children who sat long hours in the dark. Their job was to open and close the doors at the approach of workers, horses and trams moving to and from the surface.

Of particular interest to modern-day children are the stalls where the ponies were stabled. At one time 82 pit ponies were working here and names such as Abbot, Eton, Essex, General, Dragon and Tiger can be seen on the front of the stalls. There are also shoeing and harness rooms, containing horseshoes and the metal pulling gear worn by the horses, while nearby are the feed stores.

The last of the Big Pit ponies was 'Welsh,' who was a main attraction to tourists until May 1992, when he went into retirement at the RSPCA Wyndham Cottle Home of Rest for Animals near Milton Keynes.

Inside the Winding Engine House (built in 1952) is an electric winder made by the Uskside Engine Company of Newport

The Miners' Baths and Canteen opened in 1939 retains the hot air lockers for drying clothes, shower cubicles, automated boot brushes and a medical room. This is the best remaining example of such a complex in Wales.

A local mathematician estimated in 1939 that the men using the new pithead baths at Big Pit, would have to walk 150 miles a year further than they used to. The baths had been built about two hundred yards from the pithead, and that distance had to be covered four times a day - to the baths to get into working clothes, down again to the pit, - up again to bath and change into clean clothes, and then down again to go home.

Visitors to Big Pit come from as far afield as Australia and the United States and the museum is particularly popular with parties of French schoolchildren. The future of Big Pit has now been assured by its transfer to the ownership of the National Museum and Galleries of Wales and it has become the National Mining Museum of Wales.

Opening Times: March - November: 9.30am - 5pm (7 days a week)
Underground tours run from 10am - 3pm
Please phone for Winter opening times
01495 790311

The blacksmith's shop at one time had nine forges in operation, producing all the required and necessary repairs

Big Pit was the first deep mine to be sunk in Wales and opened in 1860, the year that the Urban District of Blaenavon was created and Blaenavon became a separate parish from Llanover. Today, it is no longer a working mine and has become the National Mining Museum of Wales. It is one of only two former coal mines in Britain which offer visitors the opportunity to descend in a pit cage to enjoy an underground tour.

Continuation of Walk Two

Pass below the Big Pit Visitor Car Park and follow the road past the 'Trains' sign to shortly look down on Furnace Sidings, the headquarters of the Pontypool and Blaenavon Railway Company. This is run by a band of enthusiastic volunteers who spend their spare time restoring old locomotives, rolling stock and providing steam rides for visitors.

The line originally ran from Brynmawr to Pontypool and the northern section (opened in December 1869) was once operated by the London and North Western Railway (later the LMS) down as far as Abersychan and Talywain where it joined the Great Western Railway down to Pontypool, and so on down to Newport. In 1941 the line closed to passengers, but the section from Blaenavon to Pontypool was used for the transport of coal from Big Pit and other local mines until 1980.

The Pontypool and Blaenavon Railway has been operated by volunteers since 1983 with trains running on a three-quarter mile track from Furnace Sidings, near Big Pit to the Whistle Inn. The service operates on weekends and Bank Holidays during the summer, but also on special times of the year such as Christmas and Easter. The Railway Company are planning to extend the line to Blaenavon High Level Station and are proud of the fact that this is the highest standard gauge railway in preservation in England and Wales. It also has a steeper continuous gradient than any other line.

On a summer weekend you can catch a train from here to the Whistle Inn at Garn-yr-erw, but if you prefer to walk, leave the road and head across to a gate on the left to follow a waymarked track. Across to the right now can be seen Garn-yr-erw village and above it are the distinctive spoil heaps of past industry, a major feature of the World Heritage site as a cultural landscape. Go over a stile and pass Ty Reinallt, a ruined farmhouse which had to be abandoned in 1967 as a result of subsidence caused by underground workings. Cross another stile and follow the track now curving around to the right to reach a metal ladder stile spanning a stone wall. Turn right and go down to the Whistle Inn.

The Whistle Inn was once owned by John Griffith Williams who was known as 'Shoni the Whistle'. He was a large man with a powerful personality, who fathered 21 children. When the 21st died, another child was born soon afterwards and a local humourist described him as 'having 21 children twice.' He also owned 'The Racehorse' and the 'Waunafon Inn'.

J. G. Williams was one of Shoni the Whistle's twenty-one children and he became a very successful Blaenavon businessman. He erected the town's first residential hotel (The Lion), the first brewery, the first pottery (now an inn called 'The Pottery') and the first market, which was situated in Market Street.

The Whistle Inn, Garn-yr-erw

To the left of the Whistle Inn is a large expanse of peat bog called Waun Afon. It contains the remains of a Halifax bomber which crashed here on 22nd May 1945 whilst on a training flight. Fortunately no one was killed for the crew all managed to bale out safely before the plane came down.

Above Garn-yr-erw, below Coity Mountain used to stand the Milfraen Colliery which was sunk in about 1865. The shaft was 240 metres deep and the colliery is mainly remembered for the disaster in July 1929, when an explosion caused the death of eight men and five others were injured. The accident occurred at 8.30am, soon after the morning shift had started work. Sixty-five men were in the pit at the time, but all that was experienced by those outside the actual explosion area was a rush of wind and a cloud of dust.

The rescue party found four bodies lying within a space of two hundred yards, about three-quarters of a mile from pit bottom. They also found a pit pony which somehow had survived the explosion.

At the inquest it was decided that inadequate ventilation had caused the accident. The jury also found that ignition was produced by defects in the coal-cutting machine and blamed the manager or other responsible individuals for faulty supervision. It was recommended that one oil safety lamp should be issued for each working face; that the coal-cutting machine should be examined more frequently and that a better method of searching men for matches etc., before they proceeded to their work should be adopted. The colliery closed in 1930.

As you cross the bridge over the railway line, look to the left to see the early beginnings of the Afon Lwyd, which has its source a short distance to the north west of here. **Shortly, go through a gate on the right to follow a track around the north side of the Garn lakes.**

The Garn Lakes have been established in recent years at the Kays and Kears reclamation site by the privatised coal and mining company Celtic Energy (formerly British Coal Opencast) in conjunction with Torfaen County Borough Council. The park lies on 148 acres of reclaimed land, formerly a coal mining tip. During the project 320,000 tonnes of coal were recovered as part of the reclamation scheme to deal with contamination and create the lakes. Thirty thousand trees and shrubs have been planted along with 100 acres of grassland. One lake provides a wildlife habitat while the other is available for fishing and noiseless water sports. Species of wild birds to be seen here include Dipper, Stonechat, Skylark, Yellow Hammer, Willow Warbler, Lapwing, Snipe, Redshank, Windchat, Wheatear and Whitethroat. The Garn Lakes project won a Civic Trust Award in 2001.

Follow the track, keeping on the upper path to pass above the two lakes. Then go up a track on the left to reach Garn-yr-erw village. Continue along a road past a long satellite dish decorated terrace (Lower Garn Terrace). Turn right at a T junction and head up to the Blaenavon-Brynmawr Road to follow the pavement. Shortly on the left is passed the site of a terrace of cottages known as the Black Ranks demolished in 1980.

147

On the north side of the Brynmawr road at Garn-yr-erw a row of houses, built by the Blaenavon Company, was known as the Black Ranks, because the exteriors of the houses were coated black with pitch, to protect them from the weather but at the same time giving them a very sombre appearance. Another popular local name for these houses was 'Sheepshead Row' derived from the stable doors in the front porches where the heads of people sitting on chairs, watching the world go by, would often be seen. The houses were demolished in 1980 after three years of uncertainty over their future, and the inhabitants moved to Council houses in Blaenavon.

Above Garn-yr-erw the ruins of the Powder Magazine (c.1850) where gunpowder, used for blasting in the Blaenavon Company's mines was stored (SO 246096)

Follow the pavement, passing on the right the old Garn-yr-erw School which opened in 1894 and closed in July 1971. This village was once a compact little community with its own church and chapel, its own co-op shop and post office, while the Welfare Hall was one of the first in Wales and erected by the old Miners' Welfare scheme.

In November 1936 King Edward VIII during his tour of depressed areas in the South Wales Valleys, briefly visited Blaenavon and had lunch in the Garn-yr-erw Welfare Hall. He gravely listened to the unemployment concerns of the local people and uttered his now famous words, "Something must be done for you". He abdicated a few weeks later!

Just after passing a bus shelter turn right down the road which is signposted to the Ironworks and Big Pit to shortly pass on the right the Kays and Kears Industrial Estate. Follow the pavement all the way back to the Ironworks Car Park.

The area around Blaenavon is one of the finest examples in the world of a landscape created by coalmining and ironmaking in the late eighteenth and nineteenth centuries. The parallel development of these industries was one of the key dynamic forces of the world's first Industrial Revolution, and South Wales was among its leading centres.

World Heritage Industrial Landscape
Nomination Document 2000

The landscapes to the north of Blaenavon Ironworks comprise one of the area's most precious historical monuments. It is possible within this area to gain an understanding of the ways in which all the raw materials necessary for making iron were obtained - coal, iron ore, fireclay and limestone. The areas around Garn-yr-erw, Pwll-du and Pen-ffordd-goch appear at first sight to be wholly disordered, to be nothing more than random dumps of soil. However, closer examination reveals evidence of the earliest periods of mining and quarrying in the area, phased relationships, and patterns of mineral extraction over several generations. Coal, fireclay and iron ore nodules were found together in the coal measures of the Afon Lwyd valley and the mountain top. Limestone was brought from the escarpment on the north side of Pwll-Du and the Blorenge.

World Heritage Industrial Landscape
Nomination Document 2000

THE EXTRACTION OF RAW MATERIALS

This spot and its vicinity produce abundance of iron, with coal and limestone and every article for smelting the ore; the veins lie in the adjacent rocks, under strata of coal, and are from three and a half to seven or eight inches in thickness; they differ in richness, but yield, upon an average, not less than forty pounds of pig iron to one hundred weight of ore.

Archdeacon Coxe 1801

It is possible that ironstone working took place near Pen-ffordd-goch as early as 1325 to supply forges within the lordship of Abergavenny and by the late 16th century, Richard Hanbury, a Sussex ironmaster, who was operating charcoal blast furnaces near Pontypool, was mining ironstone on Elgam Hill above Blaenavon. The Hanbury family leased the rights for a large area of common land within the Abergavenny lordship from 1675 until 1786 when John Hanbury neglected to renew the contract at the expiry date. The lease was quickly taken up by the three entrepreneurs, Hill, Hopkins and Pratt, from the Midlands of England and with the development of their multi-furnace ironworks, the greater need for raw materials very quickly had a significant effect on the landscape above Blaenavon.

Surface mining was first begun on a substantial scale on the hillside to the north of the ironworks where numerous small coal and ironstone workings known as 'patches' or 'scourings' can be seen, particularly in the vicinity of Pen-ffordd-goch.

Thinly covered by soil, the ironstone was easily obtained by a technique known as 'scouring'. After removing an area of turf, the top soil was cleared away by releasing a surge of water above it. By constructing an earthen dam, a lake could be formed and when the dam was breached the water flowed down and scoured soil away to reveal the iron ore within large stone nodules. Thousands of tons of earth and stone were removed in this way with very little physical effort. All the workers had to do was to watch and direct the flowing water over the various parts of the workings as required.

When the more easily extracted ironstone became exhausted it was then necessary to reach even greater depths by driving levels into the hillsides in order to reach further sources. The levels were usually named after individual miners who were responsible for these undertakings in the relentless quest for ironstone and coal.

Ironstone deposits were once removed by 'scouring'. This involved extracting the minerals (which fortunately lay close to the surface) by first removing the turf and then clearing away the top soil by releasing water from above. A lake was formed by constructing a simple dam and when this was breached, the water surged down and scoured the soil away to reveal the iron ore.

> *A large pond or reservoir is dug on the Common, divers channels are dug along the Commons to catch the water and convey it to this pond or reservoir, from thence is another channel leading to the mine pits. When a considerable quantity of ore is dug the pond sluice is taken up and the water running from thence with great force on the dug oare in the pits scoures and washes away the clay.*

Early 19th century account

At Pen-ffordd-goch considerable evidence of scouring can be seen dating from some time before the seventeenth century up until about 1817

To the south of Pen-ffordd-goch can be seen numerous saucer-shaped depressions marking the collapse of bell pits which are surrounded by spoil. The name is derived from the section view of the pit which resembles a bell. These pits were rarely more than 20 ft (6m) deep and about 6 ft (1.8m) diameter at the top and widening towards the bottom.

The local name for ironstone was 'Welsh Mine'. In 1800 it cost 5s a ton and by 1830 the cost had risen to between 8s and 9s a ton. By the mid 1850s the cost reached 14s per ton and it then became cheaper to use imported ironstone which contained double the amount of ore than the local ironstone and the pig iron produced from it was less brittle.

Blaenavon iron ore was rated the best in South Wales for it contained a higher percentage of iron than any other part of the coalfield. Of the six iron ore veins at Blaenavon, the best was the Pwll Llaca or 'Spotted Pins' which yielded 35.48% iron ore and was made up of thin bands separated by large quantities of shale.

The areas of extraction were known as 'patches' and these were worked by individual miners whose activities are marked by the heaps of waste material which serve as monuments to their endeavours.

A report written in 1839 reveals that it was necessary to mine about 15 tons of shale in order to produce 1 ton of ironstone, and it took 3 tons of ironstone, 2.5 tons of coal and 1 ton of limestone to produce 1 ton of pig iron. Over a period of two hundred years the amount of mining activity which took place on the hillsides above Blaenavon was quite extraordinary.

The area north of Blaenavon Ironworks comprises a landscape of unfettered exploitation, where men and women used crude hand tools to scratch from the earth the materials which were fed to the furnaces. The landscape of Blaenavon is a memorial to a particular phase of human history; and one from which there is much to be learned, especially applicable perhaps in those countries that are undergoing large scale industrialisation. We can utilise the area to recreate the experience of the first phases of large-scale ironmaking. We can admire the imaginative insights of the entrepreneurs at Blaenavon, and empathise with the suffering and stoicism of their employees.

World Heritage Industrial Landscape
Nomination Document 2000

Carreg Maen Taro Ironstone Quarry (SO 238112) probably dates from the 1840s, and was working the Black Pins outcrop. It is shown as disused on the 1880 O.S. map.

In 1788 large limestone quarries were beginning to be opened up on the northern edge of the area, at the head of Cwm Llanwenarth (SO 251115) and on its western side (SO 247125). Limestone from Tyla was possibly taken by a very early railroad to the ironworks but from around 1800 a tramroad replaced it which led via Pen-ffordd-goch down to a steep promontary which is known as a staith and is marked on the 1814 map (S0 253101). The limestone was tipped off the end of the staith to fall down to a lower level for loading into trams. These then descended by gravity to the area above the ironworks furnaces. This route was abandoned when the Pwll-du tunnel was brought into use in about 1817 and about this date the Pwll-du quarry was opened.

A small quarry on the north western side of the Blorenge (SO 270125) was also worked until about 1850 and the limestone transported along a tramroad following the 1600 ft contour to Pen-ffordd-goch. Additional quarries were later opened up on Gilwern Hill (SO 243128 and 238133).

Sandstone was also required to provide building stone and Drum Quarry on Coity Mountain was worked until the 1880s. This picture shows the remains of a horizontal brake engine which controlled the rate of descent of the loaded trams down an incline leading towards Coity Pits.

Mining for Coal

It was in the last decade of the eighteenth century that coal began to play an increasingly important part in the production of iron, for by this time it was replacing charcoal.

Initially coal was worked where it outcropped on the surface, but when the excavation became too extensive and tended to collapse they were abandoned. Drafts and adits were driven into the hillsides and as they ran up into the outcrop they were generally self-draining.

Bridge Level was one of the earliest of the more determined efforts to extract coal in significant quantities. It was driven into the hillside above Blaenavon by the three entrepreneurs, Hill, Hopkins and Pratt, about six years before they commenced building their ironworks. They in fact drove two levels, one above the other and laid iron plateways to carry away the coal and iron ore. By 1799, according to William Coxe, one of these levels was three-quarters of a mile in length.

Other coal levels associated with local men include: Aaron Brute's Level, Grant's two levels, Jack Bennet's Level, James Davis's Level, Phelp's Level, Jim Hoskin's Level, Moses Robin's Level, Dic Shon's Level, Lewis Phillip's Level, James Rees Evan's Level and Jim Kearsley's Level.

The development of steam power allowed deep workings to be developed and, although winding by water balance continued, winding by steam engines became more common.

By 1800, Blaenavon's first pit (Old Coal Pit) was sunk near the coke-yard, above the Ironworks and also about this time, Engine Pit and Cinder Pits Nos 1 and 2 were sunk in the middle of the valley to the west of the Ironworks. A few years later Dick Keare's Slope (New Slope) was opened to the north of Cinder Pits. In 1836 Forge Pit was sunk on the western side of the valley, quickly followed by Garn Pit and Coity Pit.

Until about 1840 coal was won by the 'Pillar and Stall' system which was common practice throughout the South Wales mining areas.

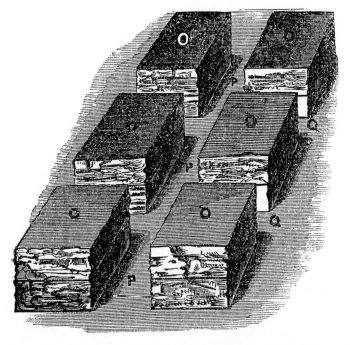

The pillar and stall method of mining involved working in stalls 8 yards or so in width, with 6 or 8 yards of a pillar of coal between each stall, with a man to each stall. They considered that if two in a stall earned 15s a week each, a man alone could earn 20s.

In 1849 Thomas Deakin of Blaenavon commended the extra safety and the economy of the long-wall system. With this a whole face was working as one operation and no supporting pillars left behind.

Reports of the Blaenavon Company between 1844 and 1855 show that competition in the iron trade had resulted in more emphasis being given to coal production. In 1850 the company even sank a new pit solely for sale-coal purposes and were anticipating an increase in demand with the completion of the railway from Abergavenny to Hereford.

Sinking a new shaft was a very difficult and dangerous job
and men were frequently killed

Milfraen Colliery, opened in 1843, was the scene of a disaster in 1929 which resulted in the death of nine men

By 1873 the Blaenavon Company were operating sixteen collieries in addition to the Ironworks and during the next fifteen years, whilst some closed new ones were also added, including Milfraen which was situated just over a mile to the north-west of Big Pit .

The number of collieries had reduced to just six by 1900 when the Blaenavon Iron & Steel Co. Ltd., were operating Big Pit (570 men), Dodd's Slope (205 men), Forge Slope (142 men), Garn Pits (166 men), Kay's Slope (382 men) and Milfraen (222 men).

Coal had become more important than iron by the 1880s and Blaenavon coal was particularly in demand for its great steam raising powers in conjunction with low ash and an unusually low percentage of sulphur. The LNWR and the GWR were both big customers and Blaenavon coal was also driving steam locomotives in India and Brazil, as well as powering big steamers sailing the oceans of the world.

Only Big Pit, Kay's Slope and Garn Pits remained in operation by 1938 and 28 years later the only colliery left was Big Pit. Within a short time afterwards, only the thin Garw seam was being worked and Blaenavon's last colliery stopped producing coal in 1980.

The Employment of Women and Children

The Royal Commission on the Employment of Children provides an insight into working conditions at Blaenavon in 1841. There were 2002 underground workers of which 26 were women, 56 girls aged between 13 and 18 and 36 girls and 135 boys under 13. Statistics given for 1838 show that during that year a total of 58 children under the age of 13 and 62 between the ages of 13 and 18 were killed in the mining industry in South Wales and Monmouthshire. It was claimed by the owners that to take the children out of the mines would ruin the industry and any improvement in their conditions would have the same effect.

Infants were sometimes carried down the mine in order that the father might claim an additional tram, but they generally started work as 'trappers' at the age of 5 years for sixpence to eight pence a day. Their lonely task was to open and close the ventilation doors to allow the passage of trams. At the age of eleven they graduated to the task of hauling and assisting in the carting of coal to the bottom of the mine shaft.

Employment in the mines from an early age tended to stunt a child's growth and it was said that one could easily distinguish a collier's child from the children of other workers by their appearance.

The evidence for Blaenavon was taken by Rhys Jones and Robert Franks and the following extracts are from their report:

Females are employed in getting the mine (ironstone) and loading it into the trams; there are also a great number of boys under thirteen years of age assisting their parents in getting coal.

The other employment for children and young persons are driving horses and tending doors for turning the current of air for ventilation, and sweeping roads. They begin work as early as nine or ten years of age.

The works do not require them so young, but the parents themselves are desirous that their children should be employed very young to tend doors or any other light work.

Girls regularly perform all the various offices of trapping, hurrying, filling, riddling, tipping and occasionally getting, just as they are performed by boys. One of the most disgusting sights I have ever seen was that of young females, dressed like boys in trousers, crawling on all-fours, with belts round their waists and chains passing between their legs.

Of the children employed at the Blaenavon Ironworks in 1841, it was reported that 21 could read and 4 could write. In the forges there were 70 boys between the ages of thirteen and eighteen. Of these 44 could read and 24 could write. This undoubtedly showed the results of the school established in 1816 at Blaenavon by Sarah Hopkins. It had become the aim of the Blaenavon Ironworks Company that their workers' children should have a good enough education to enable them to read the Bible and newspapers.

The report revealed that a quarter of the Blaenavon boys between the ages of five and thirteen were working in the coal and iron industries. Only a few of the girls of this age group worked in the mines, where both boys and girls below the age of ten, were employed to look after the air doors.

Children as young as five or six would sit 12 hours in the dark, opening and closing air-doors at the approach of men, horses and trams moving to and from the coalface. These youngsters had to start work at the same time as the hewers and remain at their positions until the last tram of coal had been cleared from the colliery. The Blaenavon door boys earned from 10s to 12s a month, which was the amount that they would earn in a week when they progressed to becoming hauliers.

> *Mary Davies, near seven years old, a very pretty girl, was fast asleep under a piece of rock near the air-door below ground. Her lamp had gone out for want of oil. Upon wakening her, she said the rats, or someone, had run away with her bread and cheese, so she went to sleep. The overman thought she was not so old, although he was sure that she had been below for fifteen months.*

Report of the Childrens' Employment Commission 1842

When William Lloyd the Furnace Manager at Blaenavon Ironworks was interviewed he commented:-

I have about 37 children working about the furnaces under my charge; the youngest are about seven years of age. I think I only have one so young as seven years; he clears the tramroad and is paid by the company five shillings per week. I have some boys from eight to twelve years old helping the 'fillers' at the furnace top, they fill the limestone barrow and assist the filler in pushing it from the yard to the furnace; they do not go into any heat or danger. There are 14 girls from ten to sixteen years of age on the coal and coke yard, they are paid by the Cokers from six shillings to nine shillings per week. There are six boys in the cast-house and refinery from ten to fourteen years. The refinery boys work in some heat in the summer time and sometimes get burned, but not very bad. There are few girls at the mines working below. They all work twelve hours and the furnaces and refineries work all night. There are only four boys and two girls working at night, they change every other week and they all take an hour for dinner and half an hour for breakfast.

The boys called carters are employed in narrow seams of coal in parts of Monmouthshire. Their occupation is to drag the carts or skips of coal from the working place to the main road. In this mode of labour the leather girdle passes round the body and the chain is between the legs, attached to the cart, and the lads drag on all fours.

Report of the Childrens' Employment Commission 1842

Rees Jones, aged thirteen was one of the children interviewed and he described his working life as follows:-

I am a haulier and drive a horse and tram in the mine-levels; I have been at work five years; I at first kept a door. My father works in the level where I drive. I go out with the horse about six or seven o'clock in the morning, and work almost twelve hours every day. There are no regular times to stop; I often eat my bread and cheese on the tram going in and out; the horse has a nose bag. I work the same time as the miners in the level, and at night, when they work at night; but that is not often. They work harder and longer the last week in the month which is the week before the pay. My father has five children, he has two girls besides me working - one sixteen, the other twelve years old; one is with father, the other keeps an air-door.

I get 11s per week for driving; I am under the Company. I have not met with any accidents; I hurt my leg by the tram a month back, but it is now well. I can read a little in the Testament, and go regularly to Sunday School. I would rather go to school than to the works.

As a result of the Commissioners' Report the Coal Mines Regulation Act was passed in 1842. This made it illegal to employ women or children under the age of ten underground. However, there was a paucity of inspectors appointed to oversee the Act and the malpractice continued. This is confirmed by the mineral agent to the Blaenavon Company in his evidence to Mr H. Seymour Tremenheere, the Commissioner of Mines inquiring into the operations of the Mines Act:-

Hearing that women were employed underground, and being desirous to follow strictly the expressed views of the directors that it should be put to a stop, he searched the pits. Notice was, however always conveyed to them that he was coming, and they got into hiding places, so that it was not until a month after he had been there that he was able to discover them. In April he turned out 70 women and girls, as many as 20 of the latter being not more than eleven or twelve years of age. He had no doubt that since then many have gone back from time to time. He gave notice that he would fine any man whom he found employing them again, and he has fined seven or eight from 5s to 10s 6d each. He gave employment to as many as he could on the pit banks; three or four orphans were obliged at first to apply for relief from the parish, and many of the men went away to works where they could take their daughters or other females underground. These men were earning in the worst times at least 12s 6d a week clear, after deducting powder and candles, and consequently had no excuse of poverty for thus employing their children. So many of the pits being accessible by levels, it was difficult to keep them out when they chose to go in.

The Inspector's report showed that even in 1850 there were still women and children working underground at Blaenavon when he observed:-

The employment underground of boys under ten years of age had also been resumed in several works by admission of the managers and their mineral Agents. At Blaenavon, the mineral agent very frankly stated that there were at least thirty out of one hundred and twenty boys underground under the legal age. So large a proportion as one-fourth of the whole is plain proof that the practice has been resumed without check, and that another generation of colliers and miners is growing up whose minds are becoming indurated by the same process of early removal from school, and employment in the pits, at the age of seven or eight.

By the time Big Pit opened in 1860, more inspectors had been appointed and heavy fines introduced, which had the desired effect of eliminating the possibility of women and children working underground. It is of interest that the law prohibiting women from working underground was repealed on 26th February 1990 which is one hundred and fifty years after it was introduced.

God made the world, but the devil made coal and hid it in the innermost recesses of the earth, that he might drive man mad searching for it.

Old Welsh Collier

Amazing Miners

Thomas Price, sinker was one of the oldest employees of the Blaenavon Company when he died in 1891. During the course of half-a-century he was involved in sinking the Garn Pit, New Pit, Balance Pit, Hill Pit, Old Coity Pit, Forge Pit, Cinder Pit, and Big Pit., in addition to several other pits in Monmouthshire, Glamorgan and Pembrokeshire.

John Henry Griffiths (86) was awarded a TUC Centenary Medal in 1969. He had started work as a collier at the age of 13 and continued in that work until his retirement at the age of 70. He had worked at several Blaenavon Collieries including Milfraen, Forge Slope, Kay's Slope, Garn Drift, Dodd's Slope and also at Big Pit, the only surviving colliery.

James Thomas Morgan was born in 1883, the youngest of seven children in a family which since 1804 had been connected with the town. He attended St Peter's School, leaving at the age of 12 to work as a colliery weighman, first for the Blaenavon Company and then for the National Coal Board. He estimated that in his 57 years in the job, he had personally weighed over 17 million tons of coal from Kay's Slope and Garn Drift. In 1953, when he had reached 70 years of age, the local union suggested that he stood down and make way for a younger man.

Eastern Valley Colliers in 1903

166

WALK THREE

Carn y Defaid and Elgam Hill

8 km (5 miles)

START: Foxhunter Car Park on the Blorenge Mountain about half-a-mile east of the B4246 on the old Llanelen road near the two tall radio masts (SO 264108)

To the left of the masts follow a waymarked footpath through the heather. An item of interest about 280 metres to the right is an old iron boundary post bearing the words 'Manor of Llanelen'. In due course a large pile of stones will be passed on the left. This is a Bronze Age burial mound known as Carn-y-Defaid (Cairn of the sheep).

The waymarked path leads in a south easterly and then southerly direction across the hillside for about 2.3km (1.4 miles) to meet the Llanover Road by the 'Mountain Well' a spring flowing into a stone trough by the side of the road.

The Mountain Spring beside the Llanover Road

Turn right along the Llanover Road to shortly pass above the site of Capel Newydd (see page 184) and after about 1.5km (1 mile) The Pottery public house will be reached.

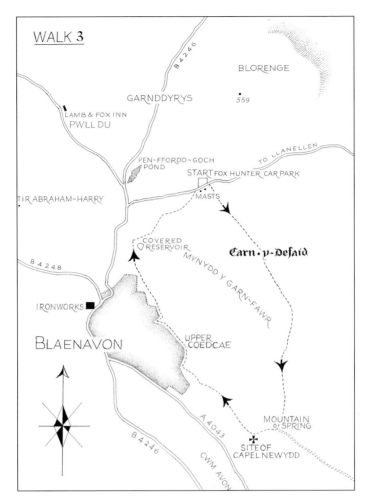

The area around Blaenavon is one of the best examples in the world of a landscape created by coal mining and ironmaking in the late eighteenth century and the early nineteenth century. The parallel development of these industries was one of the principal dynamic forces of the Industrial Revolution. In the major preserved site of Blaenavon Ironworks and Big Pit, together with the outstanding relict landscape of mineral exploitation, manufacturing, transport and settlement which surrounds them, can be seen evidence of all the crucial elements of the industrialisation process.

World Heritage Industrial Landscape
Nomination Document 2000

Carn y Defaid (SO 270099) can be seen on the north east edge of Mynydd-y-garn fawr. This prominent heap of stones is a Bronze Age burial mound which probably covers an urn containing the ashes of some long forgotten local chieftain.

This pub was once known as the 'Old Oak' but was renamed 'The Pottery' after an old pottery which once stood here

Go up the road on the right and on reaching a bend turn right by a metal barrier. A steep path then leads up to a pair of cottages. Follow the road towards Blaenavon and keep straight on at a junction. Turn right by the side of an electricity sub-station, following a tarmac lane to reach a path leading to the left behind a row of houses.

Cross a metal stile and follow a waymarked path across the open hillside, climbing steadily to reach a covered reservoir. Follow a perimeter fence to the left and then head straight up to meet an old tramroad which is followed to the right. When the track divides, keep left, passing through a landscape showing considerable evidence of mineral extraction. The track weaves around the outer limits of old spoil heaps to reach the twin aerials and the Foxhunter car park.

Evidence of ironstone scouring to the south-west of Foxhunter car park

WALK FOUR
Around the Blorenge Mountain Summit Plateau

6.5km (4 miles)

START: Foxhunter Car Park (SO 263107)

Before starting, a short detour will take you to the grave containing the hide of Lt. Col. Harry Llewelyn's world famous Olympic Gold Medal winning showjumper 'Foxhunter'. A narrow path on the north side of the car park leads to a rock outcrop where you will find a plaque beneath which lie the remains.

Follow a well trodden track across moorland in a north easterly direction to reach the Blorenge summit (559m), which is marked by a trig point and a large cairn of stones. Pause to take in the extensive view and see how many summits you can identify. On a clear day the main peaks of the Brecon Beacons will be recognised on the western horizon.

Continue along a path crossing heather clad moorland to reach the north eastern slopes of the hill. Head down to a little square brick building close to the edge of the steep escarpment. From here you can enjoy a bird's eye view of Abergavenny, the Vale of Usk, Sugar Loaf, Black Mountains, Skirrid Fawr, Skirrid Fach and in the far distance you may even pick out the Malvern Hills.

171

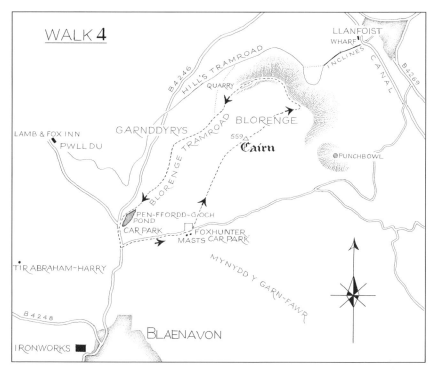

This heap of stones on the summit of the Blorenge (SO 269118) is a Bronze Age burial cairn. A cist was opened here in 1873 by a group of antiquaries but no details of their findings have survived.

Paragliding enthusiasts come to this escarpment when the wind conditions are favourable, to launch themselves into space. It is rated as one of the best sites in the country for this activity and the flight down to Castle Meadows, Abergavenny, on the other side of the river Usk must be an exhilarating experience.

Now follow the lip of the escarpment to the left. Maintain height enjoying panoramic views up through the Usk Valley towards Crickhowell. Then descend slightly to pass through a shallow gully and join an old tramroad which leads you gently across the hillside to Pen-fford-goch Pond.

This is a popular spot in summer but on a cold windy day you will probably have it all to yourself. The pond was constructed in about 1828 and early Ordnance Survey maps name it as Forge Pond. It is about 3 acres in size and was built as a header pond to increase the water supply to Garnddyrys Forge.

Later it became known as the 'Keeper's pond', after the Keeper's Cottage which used to stand nearby. The Keeper's job was to manage the Blorenge grouse moors which are the most southerly in Britain.

Abandoned and unfinished, this circular lump of stone lies on the bracken covered northern slope of the Blorenge, providing a reminder of a one time industry involving the manufacture of millstones. They were one metre in diameter and six inches thick. For some unknown reason this one was abandoned before the central hole was completed. Millstone grit is composed of a series of hard and coarse sandstones and shales, usually of a grey, white or yellow colour, and occasionally red.

Keeper's Cottage used to stand about 100 yards to the south-west of Pen-ffordd-goch pond (Keeper's Pond). It was once the home of the Blaenavon employee who was responsible for ensuring that the moors above the town were kept well stocked with grouse in preparation for the annual shooting season. During the Kennard era, the Directors of the Blaenavon Company would issue invitations to the nobility and gentry of the county to visit Ty Mawr (Blaenavon House) and join the shooting parties which always began on the 'glorious 12th of August'.

Bands of beaters were employed to scour the hillsides pushing the birds towards the butts, once a feature on both sides of the valley, but Capel Hill (named after Capel Newydd) always provided a better shoot than Coity Mountain. These moors always produced a high score of grouse and bags of 60 or 80 brace were common-place at the turn of the century. Blaenavon could boast the most southerly grouse moor in Britain. The last Company shoot was held in August 1938.

It is not known exactly when Keeper's Cottage was built but it is shown on early 19th century maps. Also marked nearby is 'The Machine' which indicates the site of a weighing machine.

During its final years,, the cottage was in the ownership of the National Coal Board and it was occupied until the late 1960s. But severe frosts resulted in structural collapse and the building became so dangerous, that when Monmouthshire County Council acquired it, along with the nearby pond, they decided that it had become a dangerous eyesore that needed demolishing. This was carried out by a unit of the Territorial Army Reserve on Saturday 14th August 1971. The site of the cottage can still be determined by the enquiring eye.

It was the Blaenavon Ironworks Company who built the well engineered road (B4246) descending the western side of the Blorenge to Govilon and Llanfoist in 1825. Before then the main route from Abergavenny to Blaenavon was the lane which starts from just south of Llanfoist (near the Monmouthshire Golf Course), and climbs the hillside past Lower, Middle and Upper Ninfa Farms. The new road up the side of the Blorenge was Turnpiked with gates erected at Llanfoist, Garnddyrys and Cae White.

Pen-fford-goch means 'the head of the red road' and it would seem that Old Red Sandstone, which occurs in this vicinity, was utilised in its construction. The red colour of the road was later even more apparent when red bunker ash from the Garnddyrys furnaces was used for repair work.

From here you may either make your way back to the starting point by following sheep tracks across open country above the pond in the general direction of the two radio masts, or go up to the road which leads back to the Foxhunter car park.

A Blaenavon man, 70 or more years ago (1830s) wanted to see the Abergavenny races, and started on his journey to that town, but when he reached Pen-ffordd-goch, near the Keeper's house, and saw Govilon and its surroundings he was staggered and amazed, and he turned back at once saying he never thought the world was so big!

Lewis Browning 1906

175

WALK FIVE

Varteg, Cwmavon and Capel Newydd

6.5 km (4 miles)

Varteg at one time was a thriving village boasting a large ironworks, several collieries, two churches, shops and a couple of public houses. The Varteg Ironworks were erected on land that was sub-let by Thomas Hill and Thomas Hopkins and operation began in 1803. During that first year 81 tons of iron were transported down the Monmouthshire Canal to Newport. Three years later a forge was erected in the valley below at Cwmavon, beside the Afon Lwyd, to serve the works.

By mid 1819 the Varteg Ironworks were in the hands of Fawcett, Whitehouse and Co., who in that year applied to the Monmouthshire Canal Company for a reduction of tonnages. On 2nd May 1820, the canal solicitor was instructed to take proceedings against the firm unless their tonnages were paid within 14 days. By October of that year the firm had a wharf on the canalside at Pontnewynydd, and were given permission by the Canal Company to run a branch from the Blaenavon Rail Road into it. This branch was taken over by the Canal Company in January 1828, when the Varteg Iron Co. was paid 16s 8d in respect of the rails and stone blocks.

Varteg Ironworks had five furnaces in operation by 1830 and the owners were Kenrick & Co., with George Kenrick as managing director. But by about 1843 the works had fallen into disuse and were advertised for sale by auction in August of the following year.

> This property comprises upwards of 700 acres of land, 227 Freehold and 482 Leasehold.
> With an excellent House, suitable for a Proprietor or a Manager's Residence, Storehouses, Warehouses, and Shops, and about One Hundred and Eighty Workmen's and other Houses.
> The Trade part of the Property consists of Two Blast Furnaces, Two Blowing Engines, Four Fineries, Clay Mill, and with a Forge and Rolling Mill, capable of turning out above Eight Thousand Tons of finished Bar and Railway Iron per Annum; and there are Tramplates, Trams and other suitable Plant for carrying on the Business of an Iron Master; and also Lathes, Machines, and Tools, adequate for the manufacture of Steam Engines, both for use on the Premises and for Sale.

There is a valuable Colliery opened, and in regular work, by Mr John Vipond, under a Lease.

The Varteg Estate and Iron Works is conveniently situated four miles from Pont-y-Pool, eight from Abergavenny, and fourteen from the Shipping Port of Newport, with which there is a ready communication by the Monmouthshire Canal Company's Canal and Tramroad; and as the Works are not of very large extent, they could be carried on with a moderate Capital, and thus an excellent opportunity is afforded for any persons to enter the Trade, both as Iron Masters and Manufacturers of Steam Engines, under highly favourable circumstances.

The Rents payable under the Leases amount to £643 15s, but there is no Royalty in respect of the Minerals raised, and consequently the Work may be carried on to its full capability without any Annual Payment beyond the fixed Rent.

Also a Limestone Quarry, held under a Lease, of which there are about Eight Years unexpired, at the rent of £36; and a good supply of Limestone can be obtained from other Quarries, within a convenient distance of the Furnaces. There are Two Cottages, held under a Lease, granted by the Earl of Abergavenny, for the lives of John Needham, Robert Phillips, Jun., and Timothy Kenrick.

The main street of Varteg consisted of 20 houses known as 'Slate Row' on one side and 'Teetotal Row', later named 'Post Office Row' on the other, when John Jeffreys was appointed sub-postmaster in 1868. The Post Office later moved to a house in Kear's Row and then to a new building on the Blaenavon Road, which also contained the Co-operative store. The last Post Office in Varteg closed in 1975.

177

Start: Park just below the B4246 near the graveyard of the Wesleyan Chapel which was built in 1868. (SO 265059)

Descend the right hand of two tarmac lanes leading down into the valley. The tarmac soon comes to an end and the lane becomes a rough track which is popularly known as 'Snail Creep'.

There are numerous hairpin bends and the gradient varies from 1 in 3 to 1 in 6. Occasional stone gullies projecting several inches above the surface of the lane made an ascent by a vehicle very difficult and years ago it often used to provide an interesting challenge for adventurous motorcyclists.

In the 1920s ascent by a four wheeled vehicle was considered to be virtually impossible. However, such a feat was indeed accomplished early one morning in June 1929, by a lorry carrying 30cwts of sand. This vehicle, remarkable for its time, was the new six-cylinder Chevrolet which had been specially prepared for the challenge by being stripped of its mud-guards and wide body and a temporary body being substituted.

It was driven by Edward Howells, a director and manager of Atlas Garages Ltd., Newport, who were the main agents and distributors for Monmouthshire. The achievement of such an ascent was seen as an excellent promotional stunt to encourage sales of the vehicle which was available with a variety of bodies at a cost of £224 to £230.

After the ascent, Enoch Williams, a professional surveyor was appointed by the company to provide a detailed and accurate description of the steep lane in order to emphasise the nature of the remarkable achievement by their vehicle. His report read as follows:-

On leaving the main road, and at a distance of 100 feet, the first hair-pin bend is met, having a gradient of 1 in 3, the roadway vary-ing in width from 13 feet to 11 feet wide, rising gradually with a slope of 1 in 5. The road narrows down to 8 feet wide, three sharp bends follow in quick succession with gradients of 1 in 5 to 1 in 4.2, the second turning being the steepest with a rise of 1 in 3.8. Continuing and at a distance of 300 feet from the main road, a gradual rise of 1 in 4.2 occurs.

Turning sharply to the right over a gradient of 1 in 3.4, proceed-ing and turning left, and then almost immediately again right crossing over a bridge, the road rises on gradients of 1: 4.9 to 1: 6.8, to again turn at a left hair-pin with a gradient of 1in 4.6, straight-ening out to turn the ninth and last bend, having a gradient of 1 in 4.3, finishing over a gradient of 1 in 3.8 until the summit is reached.

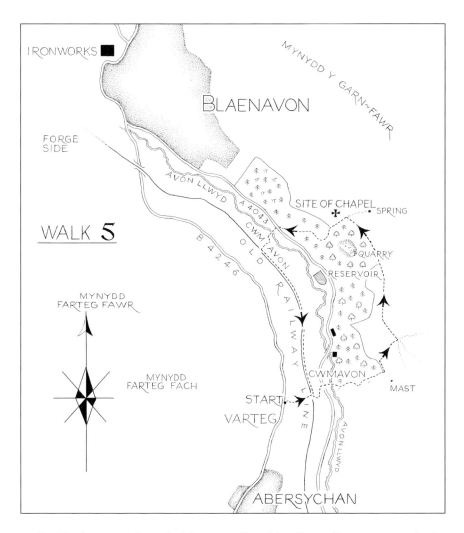

Just before crossing a bridge over the old railway line, one can obtain a good view of a group of interesting buildings in the hamlet of Cwmavon. In the foreground can be seen a five storey building which was constructed as a brewery in 1900 by Charles Westlake. It now serves as a plastics factory.

The terrace of twelve houses (SO 270065) perched on the hillside above the road is called Forge Row and was constructed by the Blaenavon Company in about 1802. Apart from Stack Square (1792), this is the only surviving example of housing from the first phase of the Industrial Revolution in old Monmouthshire.

Each of the twelve dwellings in Forge Row originally had four rooms on two storeys and an unusual feature for the time was a rear door. The 1851 census shows that only six of the dwellings were occupied at that time with an average of 4.2 persons per house. In 1975 the cottages became derelict when the final occupant was re-housed by the local authority. By 1980 Forge Row was in danger of demolition by the National Coal Board, who were then the owners. Fortunately, Torfaen Museum Trust recognised the historic importance of the buildings and purchased them, thus ensuring their survival.

In 1987 the British Historic Building Trust and the National Trust undertook restoration of Forge Row in a unique scheme which was supported by Cadw and the Prince of Wales Committee. Some of the cottages were combined to provide better accommodation, but at the same time considerable care was taken to preserve the original character of the buildings. Modern facilities such as bathrooms were of course included in the alterations.

The total cost of £200,00 was re-couped by the subsequent sale of the cottages and the new owners were required to enter into a covenant which prevented any alterations being carried out to these Grade II listed buildings.

Please note that both the forge site and the cottages are in private ownership and not open to the public.

Below Forge Row, on a small area of flat land beside the Afon Lwyd (just below the Blaenavon to Pontypool Road) is the site of a forge. It does not appear on the 1792 map of the Blaenavon to Pontnewynydd railroad, but is clearly marked as 'Farteg Works' on the preliminary survey made in 1813 for the one inch O.S. map. When William Coxe travelled through the valley he would not have seen Cwmavon Forge for it was set up a few years later.

Cwmavon Forge was most likely rolling Blaenavon iron and also some from the single furnace on Varteg Hill. It may well have been sold to Kenrick & Company soon after the Garnddyrys Forge was established. The Afon Lwyd provided a source of water power and there was easy access to the railroad, which ran along the west side of the river from Blaenavon to Pontnewynydd Canal Basin.

From the 1820s the forge was linked with Varteg Ironworks and nearby Cwmavon House (SO 270066) was built for the Ironmaster who introduced a foundry and engineering works on the site. A beam engine displayed on the Pontypridd campus of the University of Glamorgan was made here in about 1840.

Close to Forge Row is Cwmavon House (SO270066) built in about 1825 for Mr Partridge an Ironmaster from Herefordshire who owned the Varteg Colliery Group. From 1860 onwards the house was owned by John Vipond who purchased the Varteg Colliery from Partridge and lived there until his death on 19th December 1865 at the age of 59. It was later occupied by Dr Edmunds the Company Surgeon until his death on 3rd December 1878 at the age of 41. His widow, Hester Anne Edmunds and their spinster daughter lived in the house until 1909. It was purchased by the Blaenavon Company in 1918 and today is in private ownership.

Westlake's Brewery at Cwmavon (SO 269063) is a five-storey building on the east bank of the Afon Lwyd just below the A4043. It was built in 1900 by Charles Westlake for the purpose of brewing beer by taking advantage of the pure and powerful springs which issue from the nearby hillside. Designed by George Adlam and Sons of Bristol, the leading brewery architects at that time, the building is constructed in local stone, with red brick dressings and a slate roof. The 'Brewer's Journal' commented that 'the construction of the building is of the most substantial character in every way' and 'the plant will be of the most modern description both scientifically and practically.'

By the 1920's the business had declined and brewing ceased in 1928. Since that time the building has been used for a variety of purposes and is currently a plastics factory. The former Brewery and the nearby Manager's House have survived as good examples of work by a noted firm of brewery architects and have been given a Grade II listing.

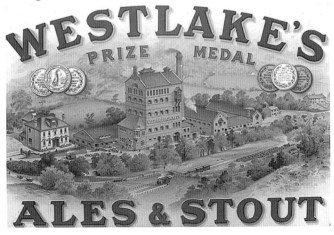

On reaching the main road at the bottom of the valley go straight across, with care, to follow the old Llanover road over a stone bridge spanning the fast flowing Afon Lwyd. The road soon begins to climb steeply and becomes a rutted grass track which is well shaded on a hot day by overhanging trees. On reaching a junction with a lane, keep straight, on now treading a concrete surface. The ascent is steep but at last it does ease slightly and at a point about 50 metres below a tall girder aerial and opposite a gate, leave the concrete track and go left to pick up a track leading in a northerly direction. After passing a large sink hole it curves to the right and heads up towards the ridge of Mynydd Garnclochdy.

When you reach a broad track, turn left to follow an old packhorse trail. This is the original route along which teams of mules carrying pannier loads of iron were led on a 16 mile journey between Blaenavon and Newport. Pigs of metal were strapped to the panniers and each animal could carry 2 to 3 hundredweights (100 to 150kg) of material. Muletrains of over one hundred animals supervised by several drivers would have been a common sight in those times.

This route was later replaced by the railroad from Blaenavon to Pontnewynydd, which linked with the Monmouthshire canal leading down to Newport.

When the first furnaces were completed the pig iron was carried on mules' backs to its canal head at Snatchwood, Pontnewynydd, for conveyance to Newport. This primitive mode of conveyance continued for many years till the Monmouthshire Canal Co. obtained powers for and constructed a tram road from the canal head to the Blaenavon Furnace yard.

T. Dyne Steel 1893

This pleasant green track provides good views and easy walking, but in places ruts sometimes fill with water, causing one to make occasional detours to the side of it. On reaching a tarmac road, turn left. Then after about 50 yards, by a prominent tree and a seat, turn left to pass an iron cross set into a concrete base, which marks the site of Capel Newydd. When it was built is not known, but it was certainly marked on maps published between 1600 and 1610 as a Chapel-of-Ease to Llanover Church. It was established here to serve the various farms and cottages scattered over the slopes of Blorenge and Coity mountains. There is a record that at one time a stone bearing the date 1577 stood in the adjoining graveyard, which confirmed that the chapel existed in the reign of the first Elizabeth.

Capel Newydd, a chapel of ease attached to Llanover was Blaenavon's first Christian Church and it was established on the hillside just below the mountain road to Llanover during the sixteenth century. Abandoned in 1861 its site is marked by a simple iron cross.

According to a local tale Capel Newydd was financed by three maiden ladies who lived near Varteg. They are reputed to have presented silver bells to the chapel but the truth of such a gift has long been doubted. It was quite a small structure and the walls which enclosed the chapel and burial ground formed a square with sides about fifty yards long.

The future of Capel Newydd must have caused ripples of concern when St Peter's Church opened in Blaenavon, for the curate James Jenkins undertook to preach one sermon every week in the old chapel. No language but Welsh was ever used within its walls and the last sermon was preached there in 1861 by John Jones soon after he had been appointed Vicar of the new parish of Blaenavon.

After it was abandoned, the little chapel soon fell into decay and stones were regularly taken from the site to repair local buildings. The last of the stones were carted away in 1893 to build St Paul's Church in Blaenavon and the old stone altar table from the little chapel was installed in the Lady Chapel at St Paul's.

No stonework can be seen on the site today where this little chapel stood in a commanding position overlooking the Eastern Valley. Congregations of farming families worshipped within its walls for the best part of three hundred years.

Head for the fingerpost at the corner of a wood to go over a stile and follow a path which shortly cuts down to the right through the remnants of a stone wall. It leads you down the wooded hillside into the valley below. Ignore any side turnings and shortly the track bends around to the right and descends beside a stone wall. On reaching a forestry track turn right, shortly passing a barbecue site (Blaenavon Community Woodland, owned by Forest Enterprise). Then opposite an old barn descend a grass track which leads down through the trees to reach the A4043.

Cross the road with care to go through a gate directly opposite and then over a footbridge spanning the Afon Lwyd. The route of the old Low Level Railway line (GWR) is then crossed and a concrete track leads up through a field. Leave it at a corner to go through a hunting gate and cross the next field bearing very slightly right to reach another hunting gate.

Now bear right to ascend a bank, passing above a white cottage. The broadening track then bends around to the left to reach the old High Level Railway (LNWR). This is now a tarmac surfaced cycle track which is followed to the left.

The oval pond in the bottom of the valley on the left is Cwmavon Reservoir which was built by the Pontypool Gas and Water Company in the latter years of the 19th century to serve the lower parts of the Eastern Valley. It has a capacity of ten million gallons. A pumping station was later added to enable the reservoir to supply Blaenavon.

A large overgrown quarry is passed on the right which once provided stone for constructing the railway. In due course you will pass between some impressive stone abutments which once supported a bridge carrying the Varteg Incline. This was built in the 1850s for the purpose of conveying coal from the Varteg collieries to railway sidings on the valley floor at

Cwmavon, which connected with the Blaenavon to Pontypool Low Level line. The incline was operated by a stationary steam engine and it enabled 3,000 tons of coal to be transported to the valley floor en route to Newport Docks.

Varteg Station on the London & North Western Railway (High Level Line) closed in 1941

Shortly you will pass beneath a bridge carrying a road leading up to Varteg. Leave the old railway track at the next bridge and retrace your steps back up 'Snail Creep' to Varteg, where refreshments may be enjoyed at the Crown Inn.

This public house was built in 1784 and became a public house in 1870. Twenty years later it was sold to the Hereford and Tredegar Brewery for £2,000. Later it was owned by Rhymney Brewery and then Whitbread's Brewery. By 1966 it had become derelict and deserted. It was under threat of demolition in 1982 but was then purchased by Jim and Jenny Rowlinson for £13,000, with five acres of land. After extensive renovation it was re-opened as a public house in August 1984.

Historic buildings in Cwmavon viewed from 'Snail Creep'

An Interesting Curiosity

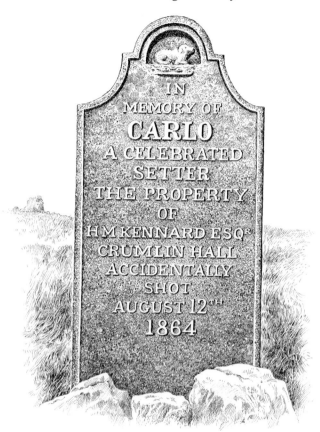

High on the south-eastern slopes of Coity Mountain, just below the trig' point on Mynydd Farteg Fawr is an iron monument erected in memory of a dog once owned by H. M. Kennard of Crumlin Hall, General Manager of the Blaenavon Works. Every year on the 'glorious 12th' of August, the Directors of the Blaenavon Company issued invitations to the nobility and gentry of the county to join them in shooting parties on the hills around Blaenavon.

The simple inscription on this iron tombstone tells the story of a tragedy which was enacted on that spot on August 12th, 1864 when Mr Kennard was shooting with a party of sportsmen on that side of the valley. After raising a covey of grouse, his favourite setter, Carlo was accidently shot. The dog's death cast a gloom over the party and Mr Kennard ordered that he be buried where he fell, just below the summit of Mynydd Farteg Fawr.

Cast at the Blaenavon Works, the iron gravestone was transported by horse and cart up the ancient bridle path, past High Meadows and the Shepherd's House to the side of Coity Mountain. Local people refer to it as the 'Dog Stone'.

PWLL-DU
The Forgotten Village

Pwll-du (pronounced by the English ironmasters 'Poolth-dee) was a thriving community. Coal, not iron was its main product: and Abraham Harry, old when Pwll-du was young, dug his drift and sent his coal to the fires of Wales.

Alexander Cordell, *This Proud and Savage Land*

Situated on a windswept hillside 1,500 feet above sea level, the village of Pwll-du was once inhabited by about three hundred people. It was by all accounts a boisterous and hardworking community with the men employed as miners (winners of ore) colliers (winners of coal), quarrymen and ironworkers. The name of the village means 'black hole' and this probably relates to the view into Cwm Llanwenarth, directly below, which sometimes when seen from Pwlldu is like looking into a dark hollow.

The main part of the village consisted of two terraces known as Upper Rank and Lower Rank which were respectively nicknamed Short Row and Long Row.

Upper Rank (SO 259121) consisting of seventeen houses and a chapel lay to the east of the Lamb Inn and at a higher level. The occupants had their own bakehouse and wash-house while the water supply for the whole community was a spring close to the mouth of the Pwll-du Tunnel.

Lower Rank (SO 245117) consisted of thirty-two houses lay beside the quarry tramroad, stretching in a slight curve from the tunnel mouth. The dwellings were 'two up and two down', ten of which were pairs of cottages that were converted into larger houses in later years. In front of the row were three bakehouses containing two ovens each, for the use of the occupants.

Adjoining the Lower Rank was St Catherine's, a Chapel-of-ease to Govilon Church and attached to it was Pwll-du School. There was also a Methodist Chapel nearby.

The Blaenavon Company had a shop at Pwll-du which was situated close to the tunnel mouth, on the opposite side of the tramroad. Later it was used as a private grocery /sweet shop. William Williams at No 22/23 Lower Rank, also at one time ran a vegetable and sweet shop.

The village had two pubs: the Lamb Inn and the Prince of Wales. The latter lay to the west side of the village right on the border of Monmouthshire and Breconshire, with a bar in each county. A stone marking the boundary of the two counties used to stand nearby, but that has now disappeared as well as the pub which closed in 1938.

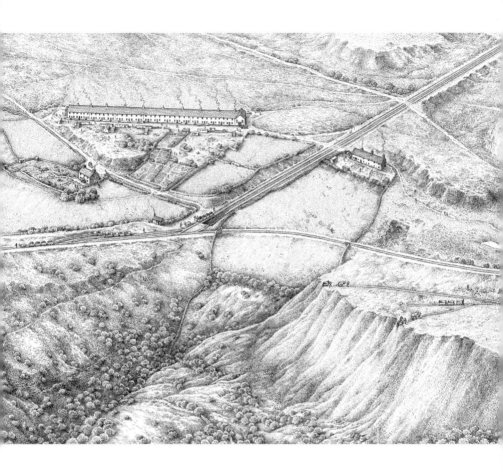

In 1960 the village was declared a slum and subsequently demolished three years later by the local council. The largely reluctant inhabitants were moved to new council houses in Govilon.

"The village has been dying for some time" said 82 year-old Tom Aubrey who had lived in *Pwll-du all his life. "I certainly don't want to move," he said. "I've been very happy here indeed. There is little social life here now, but I can recall the days when the place was buzzing with activity."*

Abergavenny Chronicle March 1962

This panorama is a reconstruction of how Pwll-du village might have been in the 1850s. Limestone from Tyla quarries was still being transported through the western portal of the tunnel to Blaenavon Ironworks. Pig iron was brought through the eastern portal for re-working at Garnddyrys Forge.

Crossing the hillside on the left is Dyne Steel's incline which was used to transport sale coal from New Pit (on the Blaenavon side of the hill) and then via Hill's Tramroad to the Brecknock & Abergavenny Canal near Llanfoist.

Just to the right of the incline is the Lamb public house (now called the Lamb and Fox).

The row of houses on the left is Upper Rank (built in 1827 and locally known as Short Row) and the curved terrace on the right of the picture is Lower Rank (Long Row) built by 1819.

Originally known as Coed Cae Crwm, the old Lamb Inn once served the now vanished village of Pwll-du. The building was erected before the tramroad arrived here. It re-opened as a pub in recent years when the owner Brian Lewis re-named it 'The Lamb and Fox'.

The Welfare Hall was built in 1940 after an initial levy of one penny per week on each of the Pwll-du inhabitants, thus providing a sum of £2,000 which was augmented by a grant from the collieries. It is now owned by Gloucestershire County Council and used as a base for outdoor activities.

The Pwll-Du Tunnel

Nicholson visited Blaenavon in 1828 and wrote in his Cambrian Traveller's Guide that 'an immense tunnel passes from the opposite side near Blaenavon and emerges upon the side of the mountain, a distance of at least 2 miles in a straight line.'

He was describing the Pwll-du tunnel which originated from a level driven into the hillside in about 1782 to extract ore. By 1800 it was three quarters of a mile long. By about 1815 the ironmaster Thomas Hill had extended the level right through the mountain with the purpose of replacing the laborious and exposed mountain route from the quarries and coal levels at Pwll-du, to the Ironworks.

The southern entrance to the Pwll-du Tunnel (SO 248099) had an impressive portal which was known as the 'Marble Arch' but this has long since disappeared. Two lines of tramroad merged into a single track before entering the tunnel. The cottage on the left is where the limestone Checker resided.

The northern end of the Pwlldu Tunnel (SO 245116) had two entrances to allow for one track leading NW towards the Tyla limestone quarry and the other for a track leading NE to Garnddyrys. The latter entrance became disused in 1860 following the closure of the Garnddyrys Forge. But limestone from Gilwern Hill was taken through the Tyla branch as recently as the General Strike of 1926.

The tunnel is 2 kilometres (1.2 miles) in length and high enough for the passage of horse drawn trams. Following a sweeping curve through Mynydd Garn Fawr this was the longest tunnel on any British horse-drawn tramroad and it was heavily used for about forty years. Horse-drawn trams were hauled from the Blaenavon Ironworks through this tunnel en route to the Garnddyrys Forge. Coal and limestone were also taken back to feed the furnaces at Blaenavon. From the Blaenavon end there is a vertical rise of 21 metres (70 feet) and from the summit it drops to Pwll-du (SO 248099 to SO 245116).

There were two entrances at the Pwll-du end; one to accommodate the tramroad leading to the Tyla limestone quarries and the other for the route leading to the Garnddyrys Forge. This northern entrance became disused in 1860 following the closure of the Garnddyrys Forge after it was relocated on the Coity side of Blaenavon.

In the 1920s the tunnel was still used for the transport of limestone from Gilwern Hill to the works at Forgeside. Each journey from Pwll-du consisted of fifteen to twenty tramloads of limestone with about 7 tons contained in each tram.

Signals to the operators of the stationary engines hauling the trams were transmitted along battery-operated bell wires. One tap signified stop, two taps meant easing-off and three taps signified go. A stationary haulage engine was situated at the northern end of Long Row and provided a 'tail' for the main engine at the Blaenavon tunnel entrance.

During the 1920s, William Watkins, who lived at No 18 Long Row operated the Pwll-du engine and at the Blaenavon end of the tunnel John Powell was in charge. He was badly disabled, having lost both his legs in an accident.

There was a locomotive shed, at Tyla, which housed three small locomotives, including the narrow-gauge saddle tank named 'Llanfoist'.

To the east of the Pwll-du tunnel mouth were situated two stable blocks, built at right angles to each other and into the sloping ground. They housed the quarry horses and the larger of the two blocks was partitioned down the centre, providing stalls for six large horses on each side. They worked in the quarry, hauling loads up to the trucks on the single-track narrow gauge railway linking the quarries with the tunnel.

The ostler lived in Tunnel House, which was situated near the stables. Close by was a pond in which the horses were washed down at the end of each day by one of the stable boys.

It is said that when the ladies of Pwll-du wished to visit Blaenavon to do their shopping, they sometimes shortened their journey by riding in trams through the tunnel particularly when the weather was bad. John Powell who worked the stationary engine at the Blaenavon end, would take special care to delay the trams if he saw any Pwll-du women approaching the tunnel for the return journey to their village.

In 1933 the tunnel was considered as a possible colliery. A heading was driven by about fifteen men working for the Blaenavon Company and high quality steam coal was found in a seam 0.6 - 0.9 metres (2 - 3ft) thick. But faults, the presence of water and possible proximity of older disused workings finally brought the mining venture to a close.

In December 1994 the areas around the northern and southern tunnel entrances were scheduled as ancient monuments by Cadw. The interior of the tunnel is currently being investigated by members of the Pwll-du Tram Tunnel Research and Exploration Group (TREG).

This picture taken in 1890 depicts some of the quarrymen who worked at Gilwern Hill. The man standing in the centre, wearing a bowler hat was Phil Williams, the engineering manager for the Blaenavon Company. In the background can be seen a 3ft-gauge locomotive and a line of trams which were used to transport the limestone to Blaenavon Ironworks via the Pwlldu tunnel.

Tyla Quarry was the original limestone source for the Blaenavon Ironworks and this was transported by tramroad from around 1800. This replaced a railroad and the route is shown on a plan dated 1819.

From c1880 two 3ft-gauge locomotives worked Gilwern Hill quarry on a new mineral line which replaced the tramroad from Tyla. This one was called 'Llanfoist'. The other was known as the 'coffee pot' and was probably a saddle tank engine, which hauled the trucks from the quarry to a point along the line known as 'Jubilee parting'. At this point a larger locomotive would pick up the laden trams from the smaller engines and take these to the Pwll-du stationary engine. It would then return to the 'Jubilee parting' with empty trams for the smaller locomotives to take on their return trips to the quarry. These operations ceased when the quarry closed in 1926.

'The Blaenafon' was constructed at Newport in 1849 at a cost of £825. The above drawing shows just one of the many general-purpose steam locomotives operated by the Blaenavon Company, which had its own Waggon Shop for making and maintaining rolling stock. There was also a Locomotive Shed in which repairs were carried out to the engines.

Thomas Dyne Steel, born in Abergavenny in 1822, was one of the sons of the Blaenavon Company's first surgeon and physician, who had large practices in Monmouthshire and Breconshire

At the age of seventeen, Thomas, who had set his heart on becoming an engineer, was working for J. H. Rende on the design and construction of railroads at Newport and Pontypool. This work experience no doubt led to his appointment in 1848, at the age of 26, as Assistant Manager and Engineer at the Blaenavon Ironworks and Manager of the Blaenavon Company's sale coal collieries. He resided at Pwll-du and his duties were many and varied. The local collieries and quarries were under his direct control, and also the tramroad to Llanfoist Wharf and the new road to Govilon.

At Blaenavon, his duties involved general supervision above and underground, especially to ensure that coal was brought in a clean state to the cokeyard and that the ironstone for the kilns was free from shale and dirt.

He soon made important improvements to the transport system by altering the cast-iron tramroads worked by horses into wrought-iron locomotive roads. Also he designed and organised the construction of the first locomotive engine to be used at the Blaenavon works. Thomas Dyne Steel recorded that 'it was the first locomotive of the hills and took the place of 25-30 horses.'

Before long a second locomotive was constructed and Thomas was also engaged in similar projects at neighbouring works. For example he was engaged by Crawshay Bailey to convert the Llangattock tramroad from Brynmawr to the Llangattock Quarries into a locomotive line.

In 1853 he resigned his position with the Blaenavon Company to become a partner in an engine and boiler works at Newport, constructing engines, boilers, pumps, iron bridges and piers.

He afterwards became the manager of Tillery Collieries (near the town of Abertillery) for several years and was also employed as Agent to Crawshay Bailey. In about 1865 he set himself up as an independent engineer at Newport, specialising in iron bridges and roofs. He died in 1898.

The Dyne Steel Incline

Thomas Dyne Steel (1822-90) is best remembered for the construction of a double incline in about 1850. Writing in 1893, he described the operation of his double incline as follows:

Each incline was half a mile long; four lines of rails were laid 4ft 8 1/2 in gauge. Four boiler plate trucks were constructed each of considerable strength and each capable of taking 4 trams of coal. An engine and drums with 4 wire ropes at the summit completed the plant. The mode of working was as follows:

One truck was say ready loaded at the pit. Two trucks were on the summit, one with full trams and one with empties and the truck at the bottom of Pwll-du loaded with empties. In this position and on receipt of a bell signal the engine set in motion all four trucks at once. On arrival at the top the two trucks crossed over ready to descend the inclines and those at the bottom were loaded at the pit and unloaded at Pwll-du. On one occasion a truck through carelessness was allowed to slip over the top without a rope attached on the Blaenavon side. It dashed down the incline at fearful velocity and kept the road all the way in spite of efforts made by some platelayers to throw it off by casting sleepers on the line. At the bottom it cut through an embankment 25 to 30 feet wide and 3 ft to 4ft 6 in deep and half buried itself at the foot. Such was the strength of the truck. By help of a spare set of wheels and axle it was got up and at work again next day.

The southern slope of the incline is mainly intact, but somewhat boggy towards the bottom. On the ridge summit can be seen the ruins of a stone building which once housed the winding engine and drum.

Unfortunately the incline on the Pwll-du side has been largely destroyed by lorries taking coal out of the open cast site during the 1940s. It is of interest that Thomas Dyne Steel also subsequently built an incline to provide a connection from the old Blaenavon Ironworks to the Low Level railway station.

From the Lamb and Fox Inn the incline descends between buildings and walls to join Hill's Tramroad.

Opencast Mining at Pwll-du

Surface mining for coal was begun at Pwll-du in November 1941 using large earthmoving equipment that had originated in the USA. An output of 1.3 million tons was achieved in 1942, which rose to a peak of 8.65 million tons in 1944. Some of the waste deposits at Pwll-du are known as the 'Canada Tips' after the assistance given by troops of the Canadian army based in Britain who provided diamond drills and the expertise needed to work them. These are believed to be the only opencast workings of this type in Britain to survive unrestored.

This was an important early development in the extraction of coal by open casting. But not everyone was pleased with the result, for in 1946 it was commented in the Pontypool Free Press, that opencast mining had reduced the stretch of mountainside between Blaenavon and Waunavon and across to Pwll-du into: 'a most unsightly landscape. This once lovely area has been reduced to a desolation beyond belief. The gigantic mechanical navvies have wrought a havoc which will take generations to repair. The original scheme was to level off the ground as work progressed, but this has apparently been found impracticable in the race for production.'

A massive opencast scheme was proposed for Pwll-du in 1989 when British Coal Opencast Executive outlined their plans for a massive operation on the hillside between Blaenavon and Llanelly Hill, involving a site of 2.45 square miles, from which they expected to extract between five and six million tons of coal over a period of ten to twelve years. The development was expected to create 200 new jobs. The then Gwent County Council opposed the proposal and after a public inquiry it was rejected by the Welsh Secretary, David Hunt in January 1993. He ruled that 'environmental objections outweigh any benefits that might accrue from the working of coal and the resultant removal of dereliction'.

If the plan had gone ahead more than 500 lorries a day would have transported five million tonnes of coal out of the site over ten years and large areas of historic landscape would have been destroyed.

However, a smaller subsequent opencasting operation enabled the creation of two attractive recreation lakes at Garn-yr-erw (see page 147).

WALK 6

Llanfoist and Govilon

7.2 km (4.5 miles)

START: Llanfoist Car Park (SO 285134)

This car park lies on part of the old Merthyr, Tredegar and Abergavenny Railway line which opened on 29th September 1862 and became part of the London and North Western Railway system. It was absorbed into the London, Midland and Scottish Railway in 1923. When the line was closed by Dr Beeching in 1953 it was part of the Western Region of British Railways. Today it is managed by the Brecon Beacons National Park and forms part of a popular cycle track established by Sustrans (Sustainable Transport) between Abergavenny and Brynmawr.

The northern boundary of the World Heritage Site takes in Llanfoist Wharf on the Brecon & Abergavenny Canal and also the little church of St Faith (Ffwyst).

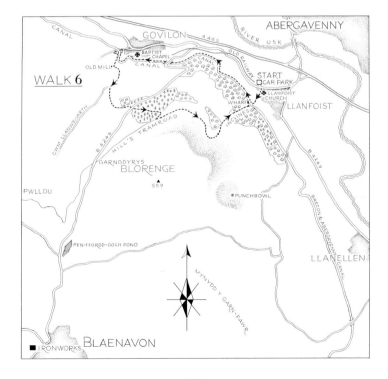

View of the Blorenge Mountain from Linda Vista Gardens, Abergavenny

The central part of the World Heritage Site is dominated by the mass of the Blorenge forming the termination of a long ridge leading down to Pontypool. Viewed from Abergavenny the steep northern slopes of the Blorenge rise in sullen splendour above the town. In stormy weather the mountain appears to frown upon the onlooker, but on a sunny summer evening when the bracken clad slopes catch the evening light, it forms a serene and beautiful backcloth.

The name Blorenge is puzzling for it does not sound of Welsh origin and is in fact an anglicised name. On some old maps it appears as Blorens and also Blawreng which has been translated to signify a grey or blue ridge.

One of the fascinating features of the World Heritage Site is that around the Blorenge one can see the transition from a patchwork field pattern of an agricultural society to the transition of an early industrial society on the Afon Lwyd. Indeed in the early years farmers worked both on their small holdings and in the early mines and furnaces of the new industry, some walking many miles to work each day up the slopes of Blorenge Mountain.

Cross the B4269 with care and go up Church Lane which is directly opposite. A stone stile on the left gives access to Llanfoist Church.

Llanfoist is an anglicised corruption of Llanffwyst and it may be assumed that the first church on this site was a simple mud and wattle structure, founded by Ffwyst a member of St Seiriol's monastic community at Penmon in Anglesey. In due course St Ffwyst resumed his travels and eventually sailed to Armorica (Brittany) where he founded the church of Llanfeust south west of St Renan.

In 1873 Llanfoist Church was restored by Crawshay Bailey Junior of Maindiff Court (1821-1887) in memory of his father, the famous ironmaster.

Llanfoist Church

This tall granite pillar marks the grave of the famous ironmaster Crawshay Bailey. Born on 24th October 1789, he was the son of John Bailey, a Yorkshire farmer and Susannah Crawshay, sister of Richard Crawshay who owned the Cyfarthfa ironworks at Merthyr Tydfil. Young Crawshay Bailey arrived in Merthyr to learn the iron trade in the employment of his uncle and made rapid progress to become a very important and wealthy industrialist. When Richard Crawshay died in 1810 he bequeathed a quarter share of the Cyfartha Ironworks to Joseph Bailey and £1,000 to Crawshay Bailey.

In 1820 Crawshay married Ann Moor. The couple had no children but Sarah Baker, a servant in his household bore him a son (Crawshay Bailey Junr.) in 1841.

Crawshay Bailey not only developed one of the world's largest ironworks, with his brother Joseph, at Nantyglo, but was also involved in the construction of canals, tramroads and railways.

In later years he also turned to politics and became Member of Parliament for Monmouthshire and Newport Borough. He was an avid freemason, who worked hard for nearly 75 years and is probably the most famous of all the ironmasters. On his retirement he lived in Llanfoist House and was 83 when he died on 9th January 1872. Two stained glass windows in Llanfoist Church.

Somewhere in Llanfoist churchyard, in an unmarked grave lies Samuel Baldwyn who made a very important contribution to the development of the iron industry during the 19th century. Born in Chepstow in 1778 he first earned his living as a printer and bookseller, but subsequently developed an interest in science. After taking a job in a laboratory at Pontypool he became a remarkable research chemist and was the first man to refine pig iron with a basic slag on a limestone bottom. He also became famous in his day as the inventor of the iron-bottomed puddling furnace which raised the weekly output of a furnace from approximately 8 tons to 20 tons.

Samuel Baldwyn was also the first to recognise that the vicinity of Newport was an ideal location for a new iron or steel works and put forward this idea in a paper published in 1859 - recommending Llanwern as the most suitable site. It was 102 years later that work commenced on constructing the giant Spencer works near the village of Llanwern. Samuel Baldwyn was certainly something of a prophet for he also drew up plans for a Severn Bridge nearly 100 years before it was built. This modest inventor was undoubtedly a genius whose ideas were well ahead of his time and when he died in 1863 he was buried here at Llanfoist, a centre of worship for many ironmasters and ironworkers throughout the iron age.

The tomb chest of Robert Wheeley who died on the 2nd day of July 1855 aged 61 years. He had been brought to Blaenavon from Staffordshire by Thomas Hill (the first) and in due course he married the daughter of James Jenkins who had been curate of St Peter's Church, Blaenavon. Between 1824 and 1827 Robert Wheeley became a major partner and a director in the ironworks which began to trade under the name of Hill and Wheeley.

Members of the Steel Family buried in Llanfoist Church yard include: Richard Steel a surgeon of Abergavenny who died on June 4th, 1807 aged 32; Christopher Steel, Surgeon, of Llanfoist who died on March 14th, 1842 aged 42; Samuel Steel of the 23rd Draggons, a surgeon, who died on July 11th, 1816 aged 38; Thomas Steel of the Royal Navy, a doctor of medicine, who died November 17th, 1840, aged 65; William Palmer Steel, a surgeon on the Royal West India Mail Ship 'Conway' who died in Kingston, Jamaica on July 6th, 1853 aged 26; Samuel Elmes Steel of Llanfoist who at the age of 34 was killed by a fall from his horse when returning from professional duty on July 29th, 1867; William Edward Steel of Blaenavon who died on November 17th 1871 aged 31 and Dr Elmes Yelverton Steel who had a surgery at 57 Frogmore Street, Abergavenny. This is listed in Slater's Directory of 1858. He was in partnership with his brother Samuel Hopkins Steel who had a surgery at 4 Nevill Street, Abergavenny. On July 4th, 1884 he took his son Dr William Steel into the partnership and the business was then referred to as 'surgeon, apothecary and accoucher.' In 1871 Dr Elmes Steel was chairman of the local magistrates. He died in 1881.

Return to Church Lane and where it bends to the left just below the tunnel leading under the canal, ascend a flight of stone steps on the right to reach the canal towpath and the much photographed Llanfoist Wharf which has previously been visited in Walk One.

In the early part of the 19th century Llanfoist Wharf would have been a bustling scene of industrial activity with the trams from Garnddyrys were unloaded and the iron products transferred to the waiting narrow boats to be taken on a two day journey to Newport Docks. Lime and coal were transported in the other direction to the agricultural markets at Brecon.

The three-storey Wharfinger's Cottage was built by the Blaenavon Company. It is of interest that the small windows in the front and rear walls of the first floor rooms were positioned to overlook the inclines above and below the wharf.

A Wharfinger was appointed to issue 'permits of loading' to other parties and was paid a salary of £5 per year.

On the right can be seen Hill's Warehouse, a long two storey rectangular building, with the ground floor open to the canal and the upper floor supported by large wooden beams carried on stone pillars, which separate five open bays. The building was positioned against a slope so that goods could be brought by tram direct to the covered first floor of the warehouse and then lowered into the waiting narrow boats though a large opening facing the canal. Grooves cut into the stonework of the ground floor related to the 2 ft (0.61m) gauge of the tramroad, but these have now unfortunately been covered with concrete. In fairly recent years the upper floor has been converted into a flat and the building extended at the rear.

The canal is crossed at this point (SO 285130) by a cast-iron bridge made up of T-section girders which support cast iron plates. In 1818 an Agreement was made for Thomas Hill to build this bridge to connect the Llanfoist incline to the Llanfihangel Tramroad, which passed through Llanfoist village. The Agreement was to last for three years and the Canal Company was to receive 3d per ton of coal and other materials or 1d per ton of lime and limestone conveyed across the canal.

It was stipulated that the bridge should not impede navigation and was to be removed after three years. Much to the annoyance of other canal users the Blaenavon Company in building the bridge reduced the width of the canal at this point without permission. The Canal Company was empowered to examine Thomas Hill's records showing tonnages across the bridge and to compare the figures with those of the Llanfihangel tramroad.

A new agreement dated 1822 was subsequently made allowing a draw-back of half the tonnage due provided that all the Garnddyrys production and half that of Blaenavon was shipped via the Brecon & Abergavenny Canal. A nominal rent of 10s a year was specified as part of the agreement.

This arrangement was transferred by Thomas Hill and his son to the Blaenavon Iron & Coal Company and it seems to have continued until 1850. But in 1853 the Blaenavon Company was sued for £153 16s 5d for the underpayment of tolls during the first nine months of 1851.

The matter was settled out of court and a new Agreement signed, dated March 1st, 1853. It settled for a toll of 1d per ton on coal, iron, lime and limestone crossing the bridge. By 1860 the Blaenavon Company no longer used Llanfoist Wharf, a railway having been constructed down the Eastern Valley to link Blaenavon with Newport.

The tunnel passing beneath the canal is shown on early maps as a parish road. It also provides access to the Wharfinger's House thus avoiding the tramroad bridge with its heavy traffic running down to Llanfoist. A minute of the Brecknock & Abergavenny Committee implies that the tunnel was in need of repair. The tunnel is 40 yards long and approximately 6 ft wide and 7 ft high - but most people automatically duck their heads as they pass through it.

The Llanfoist Inclines

High up above Llanfoist Wharf in Cwm Craf (at SO 277127) a brake-engine was situated at the side of Hill's Tramroad to lower the trams to a collecting area (just above the present tree level). Here they were arranged into order of priority before being sent down the second stage of the incline. Full trams descended under gravity pulling empty ones up on the other track which was a 2ft-gauge of 3ft lengths.

A brakewheel was set in a pit to control the descent of the trams down the incline. Passing around the brake wheel was a continuous chain which was fastened to the trams on each line of rails. Grooves cut by the passage of the chain lowering or raising the trams may be observed on some stones still in place on the incline. (The counter balance system was patented by Michael Meinzies in 1750).

In 1845 there were two recorded accidents on the incline. A young girl insisted on riding on top of a loaded tram and fell under the wheels of those following. In the same year a boy attempted to jump from one tram to another and the wheels of a following tram took off his leg.

Incline head:	SO 277126
Top of second stage:	SO 279127
Top of third stage:	SO 284129

At the two intermediate stages was a level platform where the brake-engines stood and the trams had to be man-handled from the bottom of one incline to the next - a difficult and dangerous operation.

A fourth section of incline crossed the canal on a cast iron bridge and then descended at a fall of 40 metres in 290 metres to SO 287131. Near the top of this section of incline there is evidence of damage from the canal when it burst its banks on 13th March 1860. The water flooded down, causing considerable damage and part of the lower incline was washed away. This was not repaired and there are no records of further sales of limestone in the Blaenavon Iron & Coal Company minutes.

The bottom incline led down to cross the old Llanelen road and then descended steeply, to the right of Kiln Road, to a coal yard and a set of large lime kilns, surrounded by high walls, where huge stacks of coal, and limestone were stored. It is of interest that the 1819 map shows at Pwll-du Quarries, 'limestone is worked here for Llanfoist Limekilns.'

As you follow the canal towpath towards Govilon you will see a number of level platforms cut into the steep slope of the wooded hillside above. These were made by charcoal burners who were once very active in this area.

The complete process of charcoal burning took four days. During that time the charcoal burner lived in a tent by the side of his fire for he had to keep an eye on it at all times.

On the first day he selected his site and after levelling the ground and clearing away undergrowth and brambles, he marked out a circle about 25 feet in diameter and erected a five foot pole in the centre. Around this he set up lengths of 'cordwood', that the woodcutters had left on one side for him. These were the 'remainders' that were no use to them, but ideal for his purpose.

It took seven hours to build the pile of wood and then it had to be covered with a layer of turf. Finally it had to be covered with earth. A flue was left clear in the centre and the fire was lit inside by tipping burning charcoal down it. This was then sealed with a lead lid and covered with earth.

The charcoal burner had to watch his smouldering mound through day and night, for it had to be tended every couple of hours. If the wood appeared to be burning more fiercely in one part of the mound then this spot had to be covered with a few spadefuls of soil. It was essential for the fire to burn very slowly.

Gradually the pile sank and by the end of the fourth day it should have burnt itself out and was ready to be opened. Inside were the fruits of his labour - hard black sticks of charcoal which he raked out and put into sacks ready for collection.

A ton of wood would yield about 2cwt of charcoal and sixteen sacks of charcoal were required to produce one ton of pig iron. An acre of woodland was only sufficient to supply enough charcoal to enable a mere three tons of iron to be produced. By the last decade of the eighteenth century coal began to play an increasingly important part in the production of iron as a result of the work of Abraham Darby. It was he who in 1735 successfully used coal, converted into coke, as a fuel for his Coalbrookdale Works in Shropshire.

As we have seen the change-over to using coal was a gradual affair. Many furnaces continued to use charcoal until the 1780s and until 1784 charcoal was still used at the forge for re-working pig iron.

Situated just below the canal will be seen a large white mansion once known as Ty Mawr, but now called Llanfoist House. It was once the residence of John Chambre who married Rebecca, daughter of Thomas Price, and it is probable that he built or re-built the house in its present form. He died in 1777 and was succeeded by his son Christopher. The property was inherited by his son Francis who was Colonel of the Monmouthshire Militia and when he died in 1847 the family became extinct in the male line.

Robert Wheeley rented the house in the latter years of Colonel Chambre, but moved in 1845 to The Pentre, Abergavenny. Ty Mawr with a small estate of twenty seven acres was then purchased by William Morgan the Banker who sold it to Crawshay Bailey Senior, who died in 1872 and left it to William Bailey Partridge.

On the hillside above the canal will be seen a number of small Old Red Sandstone quarries which once provided building stone. The largest quarry is just above Bridge 96, below Fidler's Elbow, a bend on the Blaenavon Road. The stone was brought down to the canal to be loaded into waiting narrow boats and taken to the Llanfoist Wharf. From there it could be taken to Newport if required.

At Bridge 96, which is known as the 'Roving Bridge', the towpath crosses over to the other side of the canal. The building on the right just before Bridge 97 was once a pub called the 'Gardeners Arms.' Just beyond the bridge is Govilon Wharf, now the headquarters of the Govilon Boat Club. An information panel on the side of the towpath provides information about items of historic interest that can be seen near here.

Scene on the Llanfihangel Tramroad at Govilon. It was constructed under a special Act of Parliament passed in May 1811 and built by William Crossley at a cost of £13,390 for a single track carrying horse-drawn trams.

Govilon Wharf (SO 269137) was the terminus of the Brecknock & Abergavenny Canal from 1805-12, but in 1810 work re-started on extending the waterway to Pontymoile, near Pontypool. The old Wharfinger's Office is now the headquarters of the Govilon Boat Club. The Wharfinger was employed to supervise the loading of coal onto the narrow boats. In later years this building became the residence of the signalman who controlled trains entering Govilon Station.

The three-storey warehouse was built at the wharf by the Bailey brothers, in about 1820, marking the end of their tramroad which had been constructed to bring iron from their Nantyglo Ironworks and limestone from their quarries in the Clydach Gorge. The building is still known as Bailey's Warehouse and with financial assistance from the Manpower Services Commission, it was restored by Gwent County Council in 1980. The building now serves as the British Waterways regional office.

The next bridge (98) is known as Skew Bridge and built to carry the Merthyr, Tredegar & Abergavenny Railway of 1862 (now used as a cycle track). If you look up you will see a join in the brickwork indicating how the bridge was widened when the track was doubled. Walk on enjoying fine views to the right of Sugar Loaf and Pen Cerrig Calch.

The towpath soon rises up to meet two bridges; the first provided in recent years for pedestrian use and the second to carry a road. You may like to make a detour over the pedestrian bridge and go down the road to visit Llanwenarth Baptist Chapel.

The Baptist Chapel on Station Road, Govilon (SO 266136), was founded in 1695 on land donated by Dr Christopher Price, an apothecary, of Upper Llanfoist House. It is said to be the oldest baptist Chapel in Wales and after being enlarged in the eighteenth century, it was also much altered in 1869-70. Renovation took place in 1893 and a school room was built on the side of the chapel in 1952. The original chapel was the northern half of the present structure and has a gallery on three sides and box pews. The pulpit is inscribed with the dates and initials: 1706, I.E. 1737, R. 1869, 1696 F.L., 1955. Beneath it is a baptistry which was built and financed by local man Ted Edwards in memory of his wife Margaret.

Return up the road and rejoin the towpath. Shortly on the right you will pass two cottages which years ago would have been occupied by Canal Company employees. Further on the towpath takes you over a stone aqueduct which carries the canal over a stream flowing down Cwm Llanwenarth. A flat area in the valley below this point is the site of the Govilon ironworks. It is interesting that the name Govilon is derived from the word 'gefaelion', meaning forges, and John Harris (d.1819), who lived at Govilon House is certainly known to have had a forge here. He was the son of Morgan Harris, the minister of the Baptist Chapel at Blaina. The forge subsequently belonged to a Mr Matthews who in about 1850 sold it to James Charles Hill, who after making his fortune, retired in 1870 to a house that he built near Abergavenny. He called it 'The Brooks' and it was later extended and renamed 'Nevill Hall' when it became the home of the Marquis of Abergavenny. It is now part of the Regional Hospital which opened in 1969.

The towpath soon brings you past a dry dock (on the other side of the canal) just before reaching another stone aqueduct. Descend a flight of stone steps on the right which lead down to a road.

Just below this point is Christchurch which was originally built as a chapel of ease in 1847 and was later enlarged in 1860 and dedicated to St Catherine.

Christchurch consists of a chancel, nave, north aisle, south porch and a western tower containing one bell, and a vestry. The first Rector was the Rev George Grove BA of Christ's College, Cambridge. A Lady Chapel was established in the north aisle in 1977 and interestingly contains an altar and cross which once belonged to the little church at Pwll-du.

Before 1865 Govilon was part of the parish of Llanwenarth Ultra. On the other side of the river Usk is St Peter's Church in Llanwenarth Citra, which lay in the northern part of the parish. Parishioners used to cross the river by ferry every Sunday to worship in St Peter's Church. (The ferry closed in 1955). When Govilon became a separate parish, the first rector, Rev George Grove had the Chapel of Ease enlarged. He also built the first Rectory (1867), the Church Hall and a school chapel at Pwll-du.

Turn left to pass under the stone aqueduct and then go up a flight of stone steps on the left to cross a stile and follow a path on the other side of the canal. Soon you are looking down on the dry dock (SO 263136), previously passed. On reaching a finger post keep low and descend to river level to cross it on a footbridge. Walk through a meadow, bearing slightly right and ascend the bank on the other side following a path heading diagonally left up to a finger post and stile. Turn left along the road and on reaching a junction turn right to cross a stone bridge spanning the old railway line. Keep right and then straight on at the next junction to follow a narrow lane.

On reaching a white cottage (Mount Pleasant) on the left, go up a lane behind it. This takes you steadily up through the woods to pass a solitary cottage on the left. The lane then bends to the left beside tumbled stone walls and levels out for a while, providing a chance to enjoy the fine views across the Usk Valley. It then goes up steeply to meet the Blaenavon Road. Cross the road with care to take the left of two tracks (over a stile) which leads you up through a conifer wood. This may provide welcome shade on a hot day. A steady ascent leads you up through what seems quite a long wood to reach a stile. Then go straight up to shortly join Hill's Tramroad and turn left.

In due course you will reach a shallow cutting which leads to a tunnel. Follow a path over the top and continue around the side of the Blorenge into the head of Cwm Craf. The path leads down beside a fence to reach a stile. Head across the next field to enter a wood and then down beside the old Llanfoist Inclines which lead you steeply down to Llanfoist Wharf. Go through the tunnel which takes you under the canal to reach Church Lane and follow it down to your starting point on the other side of the B4246.

* * * * * * * * * * * * *

This book has sought to provide information on the many parts of the Blaenavon Industrial Landscape World Heritage Site and offers six walks to help visitors explore and enjoy the special character of this remarkable area. I hope that it proves to be of educational value and a good companion.

Chris Barber 2002

GENERAL INFORMATION

Tourist Information Centres

Blaenavon TIC (Ironworks)
Tel: 01495 792615
(Open April - October inclusive)

Abergavenny TIC (Bus Station)
Tel: 01873 857588
(Open all year)

Tourism Section,
Torfaen County Borough Council
Tel: 01633 648082
www.world-heritage-blaenavon.org.uk

Brecon Beacons National Park
Brecon Head Office
Tel: 01874 623116

Abergavenny Information Centre
Tel: 01873 853254
(Open April - October inclusive)

British Waterways

Area Office, Govilon Wharf
Tel: 01873 830328

Goytre Wharf Heritage, Activity and Study Centre
Tel: 01873 881069 (Open all year).
www.britishwaterways.co.uk.

Car Parks and Access Points

Blaenavon Ironworks	SO 249091
Keepers Pond	SO 255107
Pwll-du hardstanding	SO 246114
Foxhunter	SO 263107

Museums and Attractions

Blaenavon Ironworks
Open daily to public April - end of October. Monday to Friday 9.30am - 4.30pm; Saturday 10am - 5pm; Sunday 9.30am - 4.30pm.

Big Pit National Mining Museum
Tel: 01495 790311
Please telephone for opening times between December and February. Open daily between 9.30am and 5.00pm from the beginning of March to the end of November. Underground tours begin at 10.00am and run at regular intervals. The last tour every day begins at 3.30pm.
        www.nmgw.ac.uk.

Pontypool & Blaenavon Railway
Tel: 01495 792263
Situated just off the B4248 between Blaenavon and Brynmawr.
Trains run every Sunday and Bank Holiday Mondays from Easter to the last Sunday in September plus the first Saturday of certain months. Departures every half hour from: 11.30 till 4.30pm.
        www.pontypool-and-blaenavon.co.uk

Pontypool Museum
Tel: 01495 790311
Exhibitions telling the story of the Eastern Valley, including Blaenavon.

FURTHER READING

Atkinson, M., *Blaenafon Ironworks: A Guide to its History and Technology* (1983)

Barber, C. & Blackmore, M., *Portraits of the Past* (1997)

Barber, C., *Cordell Country* (1985)

Barber, C., *Walks in Cordell Country* (1996)

Barber, C., *Eastern Valley - The Story of Torfaen* (2000)

Bowen, R., *Blaenavon in Old Picture Postcards*,(1982)

Bradney, J. A., *History of Monmouthshire: the Hundred of Abergavenny* (1906 & 1992)

Browning, L., *A Brief History of Blaenavon, Monmouthshire* (1906)

Byles, A., *The History of the Monmouthshire Railway and Canal Company* (1982)

Cordell, A., *Rape of the Fair Country*,(1959)

Cordell, A., *This Proud and Savage Land* (1987)

Coxe, W., *An Historical Tour in Monmouthshire* (1801)

Clarke, A., *The Story of Monmouthshire* Vol I (1961), Vol II (1979)

Davies, E. J., *The Blaenavon Story* (1975)

Evans, C.J.O., *Monmouthshire, its History and Topography* (1953)

Evans, E. W., *Miners of South Wales* (1961)

Foster, B., *A Tribute to the Eastern Valley Colliers and Miners* (1999)

Gale, W. K.V. *Iron and Steel* (1969)

Gladwin, D.D. & J.M., *The Canals of the Welsh Valleys and their Tramroads* (1991)

Grey Davies, T., *Blaenavon and Sydney Gilchrist Thomas* (1978)

Hadfield, C., *Canals of South Wales and the Border* (1960)

Knight, J., *Blaenavon Ironworks - A Bicentennial Guide* (1989)

Lloyd, J., *Early History of the Old South Wales Ironworks* (1905)

Lewis, J., & Thomas, M., *Blaenavon through the years in Photograp*hs Vols I, II & III. (1987, 1988, 1993)

Morgan, H., *South Wales Branch Lines* (1984)

North, F. J., *Coal and the Coalfields in Wales*, (1931)

Rees, D. M., *Mines, Mills and Furnaces* (1969)

Rees, D. M., *The Industrial Archaeology of Wales* (1975)

Scrivenor, H. A., *Comprehensive History of the Iron Trade* (1841)

Shaw, M. A., *Scrapbook of Abersychan, Talywaun, Garndiffaith, Varteg & Cwmavon* in 3 vols (1983-86)

Stevens, R.A., *The Brecknock & Abergavenny and Monmouthshire Canals*, (1975)

Thomas, W. G., *Big Pit, Blaenavon* (1981)

van Laun, J., *Early Limestone Railways* (2001)

Wilkins, C., *The History of the Iron, Steel, Tinplate and other Trades of Wales* (1903)

OTHER TITLES BY CHRIS BARBER

Walks in the Brecon Beacons
Exploring the Waterfall Country
Ghosts of Wales
Mysterious Wales
More Mysterious Wales
Cordell Country
The Romance of the Welsh Mountains
Hando's Gwent (Volume 1)
Hando's Gwent (Volume 2)
The Ancient Stones of Wales (Jointly with J.G. Williams)
The Seven Hills of Abergavenny
Journey to Avalon (Jointly with David Pykitt)
Arthurian Caerleon
Abergavenny in Old Picture Postcards
Portraits of the Past
Classic Walks in the Brecon Beacons National Park
In Search of Owain Glyndwr
Eastern Valley – The Story of Torfaen

RELEVANT TITLES AVAILABLE FROM BLORENGE BOOKS

Eastern Valley – The Story of Torfaen
by Chris Barber (ISBN 1 872730 23 X – £15)

Portraits of the Past
by Chris Barber and Michael Blackmore (ISBN 1872730 05 1 – £15.99)

Rape of the Fair Country
by Alexander Cordell (ISBN 1 872730 15 9 – £5.99)

This Proud and Savage Land
by Alexander Cordell (ISBN 1 872730 21 3 – £6.99)

Hanes Llanfoist
by Thomas Evan Watkins (ISBN 1 872730 16 7 – £4.95)

To receive copies of these books please send cheques (made payable to Blorenge Books) for the above amounts, clearly stating your name and address. Please add £1 to cover postage and packing.

Blorenge Books, Blorenge Cottage, Church Lane, Llanfoist, Abergavenny, NP7 9NG (Telephone: 01873 856114)